MASTERING CA

THE BLUEPRINT FOR SUCCESS IN CA EXAM

THE RJM ELITE ACADEMY

Contents

Contents

Contents

Contents

Contents

Preface

Unlock the secrets to acing the Chartered Accountancy (CA) exams with this comprehensive guide designed to help you navigate one of the toughest professional qualifications. This book is tailored to address the unique challenges faced by CA aspirants and provides practical strategies, expert advice, and motivational insights to increase the probability of your success.

<u>**Inside This Book, You Will Discover:**</u>

1. Proven Study Techniques

Learn effective study methods and time management strategies that top CA rankers swear by. From creating a structured study plan to mastering revision techniques, this book covers it all.

2. Conceptual Clarity

Detailed explanations of complex techniques to ensure a deep understanding. The book breaks down intricate concepts into digestible chunks, making learning easier and more efficient.

3. Practice Makes Perfect

Extensive practical tips and tricks to hone your skills and build confidence. Practical tips on how to tackle different types of challenges and maximize your performance.

4. Balancing Life and Studies

Guidance on maintaining a healthy work-life balance while preparing for the CA exams. Learn how to manage stress, stay motivated, and keep your mental and physical well-being in check.

5. Mind Maps and Visual Aids

Utilize visual tools such as mind maps, charts, and diagrams to enhance memory retention and recall. These aids simplify complex information and provide a visual framework for studying.

6. Expert Tips and Insights

Contributions from experienced Chartered Accountants and educators who share their journey and insights. Gain practical advice from those who have successfully navigated the CA exams.

7. Real-Life Success Stories

Inspiring stories of CA students who overcame challenges and achieved their dreams. Learn from their experiences and adopt strategies that worked for them.

8. Motivational Strategies

Stay focused and motivated with encouraging words and practical advice. The book includes techniques to boost your morale and keep you on track throughout your preparation.

Why This Book?

Comprehensive Coverage: Covers every aspect of the CA exam, from foundational principles to advanced strategies.

Actionable Advice: Provides practical tips and strategies that you can implement immediately.

Engaging and Insightful: Written in an approachable tone, making complex topics easier to understand.

Join the Ranks of Successful CAs

With the right tools, strategies, and mindset, you can conquer the CA exams and embark on a rewarding career. "Mastering CA " is your essential companion on this journey, providing the guidance and support you need to achieve your goals.

Disclaimer:

The strategies and suggestions in this book are meant to help guide your preparation for the CA exams. While every effort has been made to ensure the information is accurate and helpful, success in passing the exams depends on many factors, including individual effort and understanding of the material.

The author and publisher do not take responsibility for any errors or omissions or for any outcomes resulting from following the advice in this book. It's always a good idea to consult with qualified professionals if you have specific questions or need personalized advice. The information in this book should be used as a helpful resource, but individual discretion is advised.

CHAPTER ONE

THE JOURNEY- THE TALE OF LITTLE SAM AND THE GREAT MOUNTAIN

Once upon a time in a small village nestled at the foot of a towering mountain lived a boy named Sam. Sam was curious, determined, and had a dream that set him apart from the other children. While his friends were happy playing in the fields, Sam dreamt of climbing the Great Mountain that touched the clouds.

The Dream:

One day, Sam announced his dream to his parents. They were supportive but worried. "The Great Mountain is not just tall, Sam; it's treacherous and full of challenges," his father cautioned. But Sam's eyes sparkled with determination. "I will prepare well and climb it, step by step," he assured them.

The Preparation:

Sam started his preparations with little steps. He trained every day, running up hills, lifting small weights, and learning from climbers who had attempted the mountain before him. He studied maps and planned his route. Though some villagers laughed at the little boy with the big dream, Sam stayed focused.

The Climb:

The day finally came when Sam stood at the base of the Great Mountain. With his backpack filled with essentials and his heart filled with hope, he began his ascent. The climb was tough. There were steep slopes, rocky paths, and harsh weather. Sometimes, Sam slipped, but he always got back up, remembering his preparations and training.

The Challenges:

Midway, Sam encountered a thick fog that made it impossible to see. He felt fear creeping in but reminded himself of his meticulous planning. Using his compass and map, he moved carefully, step by step, through the fog. When he felt tired, he found a safe spot to rest, ate his snacks, and resumed with renewed energy.

The Encouragement:

As Sam climbed higher, he found markers left by previous climbers who had made it to the top. They had carved encouraging messages on stones: "Keep going!" "You're almost there!" These words lifted Sam's spirits, reminding him that others had faced similar struggles and succeeded.

The Summit:

After days of practice and overcoming numerous challenges, Sam finally reached the summit. The view from the top was breathtaking, and he felt a profound sense of achievement. He had done it. His hard work, preparation, and perseverance had paid off. He raised his arms to the sky and shouted with joy.

The Lesson:

Sam's journey up the Great Mountain taught him that dreams, no matter how big, can be achieved with consistent effort, preparation, and a never-give-up attitude. He returned to his village as a hero, inspiring others to pursue their dreams with determination and hard work.

Just like Sam, remember that the journey to becoming a Chartered Accountant is filled with challenges. But with consistent effort, thorough preparation, and a positive mindset, you can achieve your dream. Keep climbing your Great Mountain, step by step, and soon you'll reach the summit.

CHAPTER TWO

DECIDING WHETHER CHARTERED ACCOUNTANCY (CA) IS THE RIGHT COURSE?

Deciding whether Chartered Accountancy (CA) is the right course for you involves careful consideration of several factors. Here are some key aspects to evaluate:

1. Interest and Passion

- Interest in Accounting and Finance: Do you have a genuine interest in subjects like accounting, taxation, auditing, and financial management?
- Passion for the Field: Are you passionate about working with numbers, analysing financial data, and understanding business operations?

2. Skill Set

- Analytical Skills: Strong analytical skills are essential for understanding complex financial data and making informed decisions.
- Attention to Detail: Being meticulous and detail-oriented is crucial for identifying discrepancies and ensuring accuracy.
- Problem-Solving: The ability to solve financial problems and develop strategic solutions is a key skill for a successful CA

3. Educational Background

- Academic Strength: Evaluate your performance or Interest in subjects related to commerce, accounting, and mathematics during your school and /or college education.
- Pre-requisite Knowledge: Consider whether you have the foundational knowledge required for CA studies.

4. Commitment and Dedication

- Time Investment: The CA course requires a significant investment of time and effort. Are you prepared to dedicate the necessary hours to study and practical training?
- Resilience: Assess your ability to handle the rigors of the course, including the challenging exams and articleship period.

5. Career Goals

- Career Aspirations: Align your career goals with the opportunities that a CA qualification can provide. CAs have diverse career paths in auditing, taxation, finance, and management.
- Long-Term Vision: Consider whether the CA designation fits into your long-term career vision and aspirations.

6. Financial Considerations

- Cost of Education: Evaluate the financial investment required for tuition, coaching, study materials, and examination fees.
- Return on Investment: Consider the potential financial rewards and job opportunities that come with obtaining a CA qualification.

7. Research and Guidance

- Talk to Professionals: Speak with current CAs or mentors who can provide insights into the profession and share their experiences.
- Job Market Trends: Research the current job market for CAs and understand the demand, salary prospects, and career growth opportunities.

Conclusion

Deciding to pursue CA is a significant step that requires careful evaluation of your interests, skills, and career aspirations. Take your time to research, seek guidance, and reflect on your long-term goals to make an informed decision, in this book we had made constant effort to help you in the decision making .

Remember, it's important to choose a path that aligns with your passions and strengths.

CHAPTER THREE

10-10-10 RULE FOR DECISION MAKING

The 10-10-10 Rule is a decision-making framework designed to help you consider the long-term consequences of your actions and resist instant gratification. Here's how it works:

10-10-10 Rule Explained

When faced with a decision, ask yourself these three questions:

1. What will be the impact of this decision in 10 minutes?
2. What will be the impact of this decision in 10 months?
3. What will be the impact of this decision in 10 years?

Applying the 10-10-10 Rule

1. Immediate Impact (10 minutes)

This step helps you consider the short-term effects of your decision. For example, choosing to indulge in a sweet treat might give you immediate pleasure.

2. Short-term Impact (10 months)

Think about the medium-term consequences. Will choosing instant gratification now lead to regret or negative outcomes in the near future? For example, consistent indulgence in unhealthy snacks might lead to weight gain or health issues over the next 10 months.

3. Long-term Impact (10 years)

Consider the long-term effects of your decision. How will this choice affect your life and goals in a decade? For example, making healthy lifestyle choices consistently can lead to better overall health and well-being in the long term.

Benefits of Using the 10-10-10 Rule

Improved Decision-Making: It encourages you to think beyond the immediate gratification and consider the broader impact of your choices.

Reduced Impulsivity: By pausing to reflect, you can resist impulsive actions that might not align with your long-term goals.

Clarity and Perspective: It helps you gain clarity on what truly matters and align your actions with your core values and objectives.

Example: Studying vs. Procrastinating

- 10 minutes: Watching a TV show now might feel relaxing.

- 10 months: Procrastination could lead to poor exam results and increased stress.

- 10 years: Consistent study habits could result in a successful career and personal satisfaction.

Using the 10-10-10 Rule can help you make more informed and mindful decisions, ultimately leading to greater personal and professional success.

The 10-10-10 rule is a valuable tool that can help CA students make better decisions about their education and career. By considering the potential consequences of the choices over different time horizons, CA students can make more informed decisions that are aligned with their long-term goals.

CHAPTER FOUR

IGNITE YOUR DESIRE FOR ACTION AND MAINTAIN ENTHUSIASM

Maintaining enthusiasm and staying motivated throughout your CA journey is crucial for success. Here are comprehensive tips to ignite your desire, take consistent action, and maintain enthusiasm:

1. Find Your Why

- Identify Your Motivation: Understand why you want to become a Chartered Accountant. Whether it's career growth, financial stability, or personal fulfillment, having a clear purpose will fuel your desire.

2. Set SMART Goals

- Specific: Clearly define your goals, such as passing a specific exam or completing a study module.

- Measurable: Set measurable targets, like studying for a certain number of hours each day.

- Achievable: Ensure your goals are realistic and within your capabilities.

- Relevant: Align your goals with your overall career aspirations.

- Time-bound: Set deadlines to create a sense of urgency.

3. Create a Study Plan

- Structured Schedule: Develop a detailed study plan that includes all subjects and topics. Allocate specific time slots for each subject.

- Daily Routine: Establish a consistent daily routine to build the habit of studying.

4. Take Action

- Active Learning: Engage in active learning by taking notes, solving problems, and discussing concepts with peers.

- Practice Regularly: Regular practice through mock tests and past exam papers helps reinforce your knowledge.

5. Stay Consistent

- Track Progress: Monitor your progress regularly. Keep a journal or use a planner to track study hours, completed topics, and areas needing improvement.

- Adapt When Necessary: Be flexible and willing to adjust your study plan if needed.

CHAPTER FIVE

Maintaining Enthusiasm During Your CA Journey

1. Stay Organized and Structured

- Study Environment: Create a dedicated study space free from distractions.

- Time Management: Prioritize tasks and use techniques like the Pomodoro Technique (covered in this book) to stay focused.

2. Find Inspiration

- Success Stories: Read about other CAs' journeys for motivation.

- Mentorship: Seek guidance from mentors or experienced professionals.

3. Reward Yourself

- Small Rewards: Treat yourself for completing study sessions or passing.

- Big Rewards: Plan something special for major milestones.

4. Take Care of Your Well-Being

- Healthy Lifestyle: Eat nutritious food, exercise regularly, and get enough sleep.

- Stress Management: Practice relaxation techniques like meditation, deep breathing, or yoga.

5. Stay Positive and Resilient

- Positive Affirmations: Use positive affirmations to build confidence.

- Learn from Setbacks: View setbacks as learning opportunities and move forward.

6. Mix Up Your Study Methods

- Varied Techniques: Use different study methods like reading, writing, group discussions, and teaching others.

- Interactive Learning: Incorporate online courses, videos, and quizzes.

7. Stay Connected with Your Support System

- Family and Friends: Maintain connections with loved ones for emotional support.

- Professional Network: Engage with your professional network for guidance and opportunities.

By incorporating these strategies, you can ignite your desire, take consistent action, and maintain enthusiasm throughout your CA journey. Remember, every step you take brings you closer to achieving your dreams. Keep pushing forward, and believe in your potential!

CHAPTER SIX

SECRET OF WRITING YOUR GOALS AND PLAN

The secret to writing effective goals and plans lies in transforming abstract ideas into concrete actions. Here's how this practice gives clarity and direction, effectively serving as a blueprint to turn intangible aspirations into tangible results also it acts as a powerful instruction to your subconscious mind, steering you toward success. Here's how this process works and why it is so effective:

1. Clarity and Focus

- **Crystallizes Your Vision:** Writing down your goals helps you clearly define what you want. This clarity helps your subconscious mind understand and align with your objectives.

- **Focused Effort:** With clear goals in writing, your mind knows exactly where to direct its energy and efforts, avoiding distractions.

2. Commitment and Intention

- **Formal Declaration:** Writing your goals is a formal declaration of your intent. This act reinforces your commitment and tells your subconscious mind that these goals are important.

- **Psychological Commitment:** The act of writing enhances your psychological commitment to your goals, making you more likely to follow through.

3. Visualization and Belief

- Mental Imagery: Writing your goals helps you visualize them. Visualization is a powerful tool that can program your subconscious mind to believe in your ability to achieve these goals.

- Positive Affirmations: Written goals serve as affirmations, reinforcing positive beliefs and boosting your confidence.

4. Tangibility and Structure

- Concrete Steps: Transforming abstract goals into written words makes them tangible. This tangibility allows you to break down your goals into actionable steps.

- Structured Plan: A written plan provides a clear structure, guiding your actions and helping your subconscious mind focus on the necessary tasks.

5. Constant Reinforcement

- Regular Review: Regularly reviewing your written goals keeps them fresh in your mind, continuously reinforcing their importance to your subconscious.

- Visual Cues: Placing your written goals in visible locations serves as constant reminders, keeping you aligned with your objectives.

6. Activation of Reticular Activating System (RAS)

- Focus and Awareness: The Reticular Activating System (RAS) is a part of your brain that filters information and focuses on what is important. Writing your goals activates the RAS, making your mind more alert to opportunities and information related to your goals.

- Selective Attention: The RAS helps you notice and seize opportunities that align with your goals, bringing them closer to realization.

7. Self-Discipline and Consistency

- Behavioral Reinforcement: Written goals reinforce disciplined behavior. The act of writing down your plans fosters a habit of consistency and accountability.

- Daily Action: Your subconscious mind encourages you to take daily actions aligned with your goals, turning consistent effort into a habit.

Practical Tips for Writing Effective Goals

1. Be Specific: Clearly define what you want to achieve. Instead of saying, "I want to be successful," specify "I want to complete my CA exams with distinction."

2. Set Deadlines: Attach timeframes to your goals. "I will pass my CA Intermediate exams by December 2024."

3. Break It Down: Divide your goals into smaller, manageable tasks. Weekly or daily targets make the process less overwhelming.

4. Positive Framing: Write your goals positively. Focus on what you want to achieve rather than what you want to avoid.

5. Keep It Visible: Place your written goals where you can see them regularly – on your desk, your mirror, or as your phone's wallpaper.

6. Review Regularly: Schedule regular check-ins to assess your progress and make necessary adjustments.

Conclusion

Writing your goals and plans is a powerful practice that communicates your intentions to your subconscious mind. It brings clarity, enhances focus, strengthens commitment, and guides your actions toward achieving tangible results. By regularly reviewing and visualizing your goals, you keep your subconscious mind engaged and aligned with your aspirations, ultimately turning your dreams into reality.

Remember, a written goal is a goal half-achieved. Keep pushing forward, and let your subconscious mind work its magic in bringing your goals to life!

CHAPTER SEVEN

DARWIN'S THEORY – A LESSONS FOR FLEXIBILITY, ADAPTABILITY, RESILIENCE AND CONTINUOUS IMPROVEMENT

Darwin's Theory of Evolution is centred around the concept of natural selection, where organisms better adapted to their environment tend to survive and produce more offspring. This theory emphasizes the importance of adaptation, resilience, and continuous improvement.

How It Applies to CA Students

1. Adaptation: Just as species must adapt to survive, CA students need to adapt their study methods to the evolving demands of the course. This might mean finding new ways to understand complex topics or adjusting your schedule to accommodate more study time.

2. Resilience: Darwin's theory highlights the importance of resilience. CA students will face challenges and setbacks, but like species that survive through tough conditions, students who persevere and remain resilient are more likely to succeed.

3. Continuous Improvement: Evolution is a continuous process, and so is learning. CA students should focus on continuous improvement, regularly reviewing their progress, and seeking ways to enhance their knowledge and skills.

4. Strategic Planning: Just as natural selection favors organisms with advantageous traits, CA students should strategically plan their studies to focus on areas that will give them the greatest advantage in their exams.

5. Learning from Mistakes: In evolution, mistakes (or unfavorable traits) are weeded out over time. Similarly, CA students should learn from their mistakes, understand where they went wrong, and make necessary adjustments to improve.

Conclusion

Darwin's theory of evolution can serve as a powerful metaphor for CA students, reminding them of the importance of adaptation, resilience, continuous improvement, strategic planning, and learning from mistakes. By embracing these principles, CA students can navigate their studies more effectively and increase their chances of success.

CHAPTER EIGHT

STRATEGIC PREPARATION A MAGIC FORMULA

Success in CA exams is more about strategic preparation which is a magical formula. Here are some actionable tips to boost your chances of scoring higher:

1.Understand the Syllabus and exam pattern:

- Familiarize yourself thoroughly with the syllabus and exam pattern. Knowing what to expect helps in efficient preparation.

2. Create a Study Schedule:

- Plan your study schedule well in advance. Allocate more time to difficult subjects or topics you're less familiar with.

3. Conceptual Clarity:

- Focus on understanding the concepts rather than rote learning. This will help you tackle any tricky questions with ease.

4. Regular Revision:

- Regularly revise the topics you've studied. It ensures better retention and helps you recall information during exams.

5. Practice Mock Tests:

- Practice past exam papers and mock tests under exam conditions. It will help you manage your time better and improve your exam techniques.

6. Focus on Presentation:

- Pay attention to how you present your answers. Structured and well-presented answers can fetch you more marks.

7. Time Management:

- Practice solving questions within the time limit. Allocate specific time slots for each question in the exam.

8. Stay Updated:

- Stay updated with any amendments or changes in the syllabus or exam pattern by ICAI.

9. Stay Healthy:

- Maintain a healthy lifestyle. Proper sleep, diet, and regular exercise can significantly improve your concentration and productivity.

10. Seek Help When Needed:

- Don't hesitate to seek help from teachers, mentors, or peers if you find certain topics challenging.

11. Positive Mindset:

- Keep a positive mindset. Stress and anxiety can hamper your performance. Practice mindfulness or relaxation techniques if needed.

By following these strategies, you'll be well on your way to achieving great marks in your CA exams. Good luck! ?

CHAPTER NINE

ABOUT THE INSTITUTE OF CHARTERED ACCOUNTANTS OF INDIA

The Institute of Chartered Accountants of India (ICAI) is a statutory body established under the Chartered Accountants Act, 1949. It is responsible for regulating the profession of Chartered Accountancy in India. Here are some key points about ICAI:

Overview

- Establishment: ICAI was set up by an Act of Parliament and functions under the administrative control of the Ministry of Corporate Affairs, Government of India.

- Global Presence: It is the largest professional accounting body in the world in terms of membership.

- Mission: ICAI aims to develop, regulate, and maintain the profession of Chartered Accountancy in the country.

Functions

- Education and Examination: ICAI conducts examinations for Chartered Accountancy courses and provides education and training to aspiring CAs.

- Professional Development: It offers continuing professional education to its members to ensure they stay updated with the latest developments in the field.

- Standards and Ethics: ICAI formulates accounting standards, auditing standards, and ethical standards for the profession.

- Quality Monitoring: The institute monitors the quality of services provided by its members through peer reviews and disciplinary actions.

- Policy Input: ICAI provides input on policy matters to the government and other stakeholders.

Resources and Support

- Digital Learning Hub: ICAI offers a digital learning hub called eSahaayataa for online education and resources.

- Self Service Portal: Members can access various services and information through the ICAI Self Service Portal.

- Events and Webinars: The institute organizes events, webinars, and seminars to support the professional growth of its members.

For more information and recent updates, you can visit the [ICAI website](https://www.icai.org/).

CHAPTER TEN

HEAD OFFICE, REGIONAL OFFICE AND BRANCHES OF ICAI

The Institute of Chartered Accountants of India (ICAI) has a widespread presence across India and even internationally. Here's an overview of its branches:

Head Office

ICAI Bhawan, Indraprastha Marg, Post Box No. 7100, New Delhi - 110 002, India

Regional Offices

1. **Eastern India Regional Council (EIRC):** ICAI Bhawan, 382/A, Prantik Pally, Rajdanga, Kasba, Kolkata - 700107, West Bengal, India
2. **Western India Regional Council (WIRC):** ICAI Tower, C-40, G Block, Opposite MCA Ground, Bandra Kurla Complex, Bandra East, Mumbai - 400051, Maharashtra, India
3. **Southern India Regional Council (SIRC):** ICAI Bhawan, 122, Mahatma Gandhi Road, Nungambakkam, Chennai - 600 034, Tamil Nadu, India
4. **Northern India Regional Council (NIRC):** ICAI Bhawan, 52-53-54, Institutional Area, Vishwas Nagar, Shahdara, Near Karkardooma Courts, Delhi - 110 032, India
5. **Central India Regional Council (CIRC):** ICAI Bhawan, Post Box No. 314, 16/77B, Civil Lines, Behind Reserve Bank of India, Kanpur - 208

001, Uttar Pradesh, India

Branches in India

ICAI has 177 branches across various cities in India. Some of the notable branches include:
- Asansol Branch: Asansol, West Bengal
- Bangalore Branch: Bangalore , Karnataka
- Bhubaneswar Branch: Bhubaneswar, Odisha
- Coimbatore Branch : Coimbatore
- Erode Branch : Erode
- Tirupur Branch : Tirupur
- Cuttack Branch: Cuttack, Odisha
- Durgapur Branch: Durgapur, West Bengal
- Guwahati Branch: Guwahati, Assam

International Chapters

ICAI also has 50 chapters outside India, providing support and resources to Indian CA professionals and students abroad.

CHAPTER ELEVEN

Overview of the new scheme of The Chartered Accountancy (CA) Course

The Chartered Accountancy (CA) course offered by the Institute of Chartered Accountants of India (ICAI) is structured into three levels, each with its own set of exams and training requirements.

The CA exam is a challenging but rewarding professional qualification. Here's a step-by-step guide to help you navigate the new scheme of education introduced in July 2023:

1. Foundation Course:

- **Eligibility:** Complete your 10th standard to register for the Foundation course. However, you can only appear for the Foundation exam after passing 12th grade.
- **Registration:** Register online with the Institute of Chartered Accountants of India (ICAI).
- **Study Material:** Obtain study material from ICAI or enroll in coaching classes.
- **Exam:** Appear for the CA Foundation exam after a minimum of 4 months of study. Exams are held twice a year (usually in May and November). you can only appear for the Foundation exam after passing

12th grade.

- **Passing Criteria:** Pass all four subjects (Principles and Practice of Accounting, Business Laws and Business Correspondence and Reporting, Business Mathematics and Logical Reasoning,and Economics and Business Statistics). You need a minimum of 40% in each paper and a total of 50% across all four papers to pass.

2. Intermediate Course:

- **Eligibility:** Passing the Foundation However, if you are a graduate with specified marks, you can enter directly into CA Intermediate (Direct Entry Scheme). If using the Direct Entry route, ensure you meet the percentage requirements (55% for commerce graduates or 60% for non-commerce).
- **Registration:** Register online with ICAI.
- **Study Material:** Obtain study material from ICAI or enroll in coaching classes.
- **Exam:** Appear for the CA Intermediate exam after a minimum of 8 months of study.You can appear for either one or both groups in a single exam session.
- **Passing Criteria:** Each paper requires a minimum of 40% marks, and an aggregate of 50% in each group.

3. Integrated Course on Information Technology and Soft Skills (ICITSS):

- **Eligibility:** Pass both groups of the CA Intermediate exam.
- **Completion:** Complete the ICITSS before commencing articleship.

4. Articleship\Practical Training:

- **Eligibility:** Pass both groups of the CA Intermediate exam and complete ICITSS.
- **Self-Paced Online Modules (SPOMs):** Utilize SPOMs for in-depth learning and practice.
- **Duration:** 2 years of practical training under the guidance of a practicing Chartered Accountant.
- **Registration:** Register with ICAI for articleship.

5. Advanced ICITSS:

- **Eligibility:** Complete articleship.
- **Completion:** Complete the Advanced ICITSS before appearing for the CA Final exam.

6. CA Final Course:

- **Eligibility:** Complete articleship and Advanced ICITSS.
- **Registration:** Register online with ICAI.
- **Study Material:** Obtain study material from ICAI or enroll in coaching classes.
- **Exam:** Appear for the CA Final exam after a minimum of 6 months of study. Exams are held twice a year (May and November).
- **Passing Criteria:** You need a minimum of 40% in each paper and a 50% aggregate per group.

7. Membership:

- **Eligibility:** Pass both groups of the CA Final exam.
- **Application:** Apply for membership with ICAI.
- **Membership:** Upon approval, you will become a Chartered Accountant.

Key Points to Remember:

- The new scheme of education aims to enhance the practical relevance of the CA course.
- The duration of the course has been reduced from 5 years to 4.5 years.
- The focus is on developing practical skills and knowledge through a blend of theoretical and practical training.
- Regular revisions and updates to the syllabus are made by ICAI.
- Stay updated with the latest information and notifications from ICAI.
- Plan your studies strategically and consistently to ensure success.
- Seek guidance from experienced professionals or mentors.

By following these steps and maintaining dedication and perseverance, you can successfully navigate the CA exam and achieve your goal of becoming a Chartered Accountant.

Disclaimer: This information is for general guidance only and may be subject to change. Please refer to the official ICAI website or prospectus for the most up-to-date information and regulations.

26

Approximate Expenses for Pursuing CA

The fees for the CA course can vary depending on several factors, including:

- Registration Fees: These fees are paid to the Institute of Chartered Accountants of India (ICAI) for registration at each level (Foundation, Intermediate, and Final).
- Examination Fees: These fees are paid to ICAI for appearing in the respective examinations.
- Coaching Fees: If you opt for coaching classes, you'll need to pay tuition fees to the coaching institute.
- Study Material Costs: Costs for purchasing study materials from ICAI or other sources.
- Travel and Accommodation Costs: If you need to travel for coaching or examinations, you'll incur travel and accommodation expenses.

Approximate Total Cost:

The total cost of the CA course can range from ₹3-5 lakhs or even higher, depending on your individual circumstances and choices.

Key Points:

- ICAI Website: For the most accurate and up-to-date information on fees, please refer to the official ICAI website: https://www.icai.org/

- Coaching Costs: Coaching fees can vary significantly depending on the institute, location, and mode of instruction (classroom, online, etc.).
- Multiple Attempts: If you need multiple attempts to clear any of the examinations, the overall cost will increase.

CHAPTER THIRTEEN

SELF-STUDY VS PRIVATE COACHING

Taking private coaching classes is not mandatory for CA students, but it can be highly beneficial for many. Here's a balanced view of both sides:

Benefits of Private Coaching

1. Expert Guidance:

- Experienced faculty can provide deeper insights and clarify complex concepts.

2. Structured Learning:

- Coaching institutes offer a well-organized curriculum and study schedule.

3. Mock Tests and Practice Papers:

- Regular tests help in assessing your preparation and improving exam strategies.

4. Peer Learning:

- Interacting with fellow students can enhance understanding through discussions and group studies.

5. Doubt Resolution:

- Immediate resolution of doubts can prevent misunderstandings and strengthen concepts.

Self-Study and ICAI Resources

1. Official ICAI Materials:

- ICAI provides comprehensive study materials, practice manuals, and mock test papers.

2. Flexibility:

- Self-study offers flexibility to learn at your own pace and focus on weak areas.

3. Cost-Effective:

- Avoiding coaching fees can reduce the financial burden.

4. Personalized Study Plan:

- You can create a study plan tailored to your strengths and weaknesses.

5. Online Resources:

- Many free and paid online resources, including video lectures, forums, and study groups, are available.

Conclusion

Ultimately, whether or not to take private coaching depends on your personal preferences, learning style, and circumstances. Some students thrive with self-study using ICAI materials, while others benefit from the structured environment and additional support provided by coaching institutes.

Assess your learning needs, available resources, and the level of support you require to make an informed decision but Private coaching is highly recommended.

CHAPTER FOURTEEN

CHOOSING BETWEEN ONLINE AND PHYSICAL COACHING CLASSES

The choice between online and physical coaching for the CA exam depends heavily on your individual learning style, preferences, and circumstances. Here's a breakdown to help you decide:

Online Coaching
Pros:

- Flexibility and Convenience: Study at your own pace and time, from anywhere with an internet connection.
- Cost-Effectiveness: Often more affordable than physical coaching, eliminating travel and accommodation expenses.
- Access to Top Faculty: Access to renowned faculty from across the country, regardless of your location.
- Re-watch Lectures: Revisit concepts and lectures as many times as needed.
- Interactive Platforms: Many platforms offer interactive features like quizzes, discussions, and doubt-solving sessions.

Cons:

- Self-Discipline: Requires strong self-discipline and motivation to stay focused and on schedule.

- Limited Interaction: May lack the in-person interaction and peer-to-peer learning of physical classrooms.
- Technical Issues: Potential for technical glitches and internet connectivity problems.
- Distractions: Requires a dedicated study environment to minimize distractions.

Physical Coaching
Pros:

- Structured Learning: Provides a structured learning environment with regular classes and a fixed schedule.
- In-Person Interaction: Facilitates interaction with faculty and fellow students, fostering peer learning and discussions.
- Doubt-Clearing Sessions: Regular doubt-clearing sessions with faculty for immediate clarification.
- Motivation and Discipline: The classroom environment can provide motivation and discipline.
- Personalized Attention: Faculty can provide personalized attention and guidance.

Cons:

- Limited Flexibility: Bound by fixed class schedules, making it difficult to accommodate other commitments.
- Higher Costs: Involves travel, accommodation, and potentially higher tuition fees.
- Limited Access to Top Faculty: May not have access to the same range of top faculty as online platforms.
- Travel Time and Effort: Requires commuting to the coaching center, which can be time-consuming and tiring.

Here are some factors to consider when making your decision:

- Learning Style: Are you self-motivated and disciplined enough for online learning, or do you prefer a structured classroom environment?
- Budget: Consider the cost of online vs. physical coaching, including travel, accommodation, and other expenses.

- Location and Accessibility: If you live in a remote location, online coaching may be the only viable option.
- Faculty Preference: Research the faculty at different coaching institutes and choose the one that best suits your learning style.
- Flexibility and Time Constraints: Consider your other commitments and whether you need the flexibility of online learning.

Ultimately, the best choice depends on your individual needs and preferences. Many students find a blended approach, combining the flexibility of online learning with the structure and interaction of occasional physical classes, to be the most effective.

Additional Tips:

- Trial Classes: Consider taking trial classes at different institutes to experience both online and physical coaching before making a decision.
- Read Reviews: Read reviews and testimonials from past students to get insights into the quality of instruction and student experience.
- Consult with Seniors: Seek advice from seniors who have already cleared the CA exam and can share their experiences with different coaching options.

By carefully considering these factors, you can choose the coaching option that best suits your needs and helps you achieve your goal of becoming a Chartered Accountant.

CHAPTER FIFTEEN

MYTHS ABOUT CA EXAMS

Here are myths about CA exams along with the facts to debunk them. It's important to separate fact from fiction to approach the exams with the right mindset.

1. Myth: Only geniuses can clear CA exams.

- Fact: Anyone with dedication and proper preparation can clear CA exams.

2. Myth: CA exams are impossible to pass on the first attempt.

- Fact: Many students clear CA exams on their first attempt with consistent effort and smart study strategies.

3. Myth: You need to study 16 hours a day to pass.

- Fact: Effective and focused study is more important than long hours.

4. Myth: Commerce background is a must to succeed in CA.

- Fact: Students from any background can pursue CA and succeed with hard work. Many Non commerce Students succeed too.

5. Myth: CA exams require memorization of laws and regulations.

- Fact: Understanding and application of concepts are more crucial than rote memorization.

6. Myth: CA students have no social life.

- Fact: With proper time management, CA students can balance studies and personal life.

7. Myth: You must attend coaching classes to pass CA exams.

- Fact: Many students pass by self-study using ICAI materials and other resources but private coaching offers additional advantage.

8. Myth: CA exams are designed to make students fail.

- Fact: The exams are rigorous but fair, aimed at maintaining high professional standards.

9. Myth: All CAs end up in auditing jobs.

- Fact: CAs have diverse career opportunities in various fields like finance, taxation, consulting, and more.

10. Myth: You can only succeed in CA if you start at an early age.

- Fact: Age is not a barrier. Many students start later and still achieve success.

11. Myth: CA exams require extraordinary intelligence.

- Fact: Hard work, consistency, and smart study methods are key to success.

12. Myth: ICAI materials are not sufficient for preparation.

- Fact: ICAI study materials are comprehensive and cover the entire syllabus.

13. Myth: Only ICAI-toppers have a bright future.

- Fact: All qualified CAs have excellent career prospects, irrespective of their ranks.

14. Myth: CA exams are more difficult than any other professional exams.

- Fact: While challenging, CA exams are comparable to other professional exams in terms of difficulty.

15. Myth: It's impossible to work and study for CA simultaneously.

- Fact: Many students balance articleship and studies successfully.

16. Myth: Failing CA exams means you are not capable.

- Fact: Failure is a part of the learning process. Many successful CAs have faced setbacks.

17. Myth: CA exams can only be cleared by studying from day one.

- Fact: Consistent effort and strategic revision closer to exams can also lead to success.

18. Myth: You need to remember every section of the law.

- Fact: Understanding key sections and their applications is more important than memorizing everything, This book had covered lot of Tips and tricks.

19. Myth: CA course is extremely expensive.

- Fact: Compared to many other professional courses, CA is relatively affordable.

20. Myth: Only rankers get good job placements.

- Fact: All qualified CAs have ample job opportunities, irrespective of their ranks.

21. Myth: Coaching institutes guarantee success.

- Fact: Success depends on individual effort, not just coaching but Private coaching is highly recommended

22. Myth: CA exams are all about theory.

- Fact: CA exams test practical application and problem-solving skills.

23. Myth: You can't pass CA exams without group study.

- Fact: Both group study and self-study have their advantages; success depends on the individual's preference.

24. Myth: Only CA professionals are allowed to audit.

- Fact: While CAs are the preferred choice, other professionals can also audit under certain regulations.

25. Myth: CA exams have biased marking.

- Fact: ICAI follows a standardized and fair evaluation process.

26. Myth: Female students have a harder time clearing CA exams.

- Fact: Gender has no bearing on the ability to clear CA exams; success depends on effort and preparation. Women are increasingly pursuing and excelling in the CA profession.

27. Myth: Only students from top schools and colleges can clear CA exams.

- Fact: Students from all educational backgrounds have cleared CA exams successfully.

28. Myth: CA is only about accounting and finance.

- Fact: The CA curriculum covers diverse subjects including law, taxation, and management.

29. Myth: Taking breaks will hamper your CA preparation.

- Fact: Regular breaks are essential for maintaining focus and avoiding burnout.

30. Myth: CA exams are purely bookish knowledge.

- Fact: Practical application and understanding of real-world scenarios are crucial.

31. Myth: Every CA works in an accounting firm.

- Fact: CAs work in various industries including corporate, banking, and government sectors.

32. Myth: You cannot pass CA exams without sacrificing your hobbies.

- Fact: Balancing studies with hobbies is possible and can enhance overall well-being.

33. Myth: Only students with high IQ can pass CA exams.

- Fact: Diligence, strategic planning, and perseverance are more important than IQ.

34. Myth: Once you fail a CA exam, it's impossible to pass.

- Fact: Many students succeed in subsequent attempts with improved strategies.

35. Myth: CA exams are subjective and unpredictable.

- Fact: Exams are based on a well-defined syllabus and pattern.

36. Myth: Articleship experience is not valuable.

- Fact: Articleship provides practical experience and is crucial for overall development.

37. Myth: CA students can't work part-time jobs.

- Fact: Many CA students manage part-time jobs along with their studies effectively.

38. Myth: Clearing CA exams guarantees instant high-paying jobs.

- Fact: While CA qualification opens many doors, job opportunities depend on various factors including skills and experience.

39. Myth: You need to remember all previous exam questions.

- Fact: Understanding the pattern and practicing past papers helps, but rote memorization of all questions is not required.

40. Myth: CA exams have a fixed quota of students who can pass.

- Fact: Passing is based on individual performance and not on a fixed quota.

41. Myth: All CAs work long, tedious hours.

- Fact: Work-life balance varies across different roles and organizations.

42. Myth: CA exams are more difficult than any other professional exams.

- Fact: While challenging, CA exams are comparable to other professional exams in terms of difficulty.

43. Myth: It's impossible to clear CA exams without coaching.

- Fact: Many students clear the exams through self-study with proper guidance and resources but private coaching is recommended.

44. Myth: CA qualification is only recognized in India.

- Fact: CA qualification is recognized globally and CAs have career opportunities worldwide.

45. Myth: CA course is only suitable for extroverts.

- Fact: Both introverts and extroverts can succeed in the CA field with the right skills and competencies.

46. Myth: Every CA job is monotonous.

- Fact: CAs have diverse roles with varying responsibilities, making the job dynamic and interesting.

47. Myth: CA exams test memory more than understanding.

- Fact: Exams test comprehension, application, and analytical skills.

48. Myth: You need to follow every book and material available.

- Fact: Focusing on ICAI materials and selective additional resources is usually sufficient.

49. Myth: CA students can't pursue additional certifications.

- Fact: Many CA students pursue additional certifications to enhance their career prospects.

50. Myth: Only rank holders have a successful career.

- Fact: All qualified CAs can have successful careers irrespective of their ranks.

51. Myth: CA exams don't test practical skills.

- Fact: Practical skills and real-world applications are heavily tested in CA exams.

52. Myth: You need to study day and night without any breaks.

- Fact: Proper breaks and rest are essential for effective studying and retention.

53. Myth: You can't pass CA exams if you start late.

- Fact: Consistent effort, irrespective of when you start, can lead to success.

54. Myth: Only top scorers in school can clear CA exams.

- Fact: Many average students excel in CA exams through dedication and smart preparation.

55. Myth: CA exams are about luck.

- Fact: Success in CA exams is a result of hard work, preparation, and strategy, not luck.

56. Myth: CA students don't need any extracurricular activities.

- Fact: Engaging in extracurricular activities can improve overall well-being and enhance productivity.

57. Myth: All CA jobs are desk jobs.

- Fact: CA roles can vary from fieldwork, client interactions, and advisory positions, to desk jobs.

58. Myth: You need to study in isolation to succeed.

- Fact: Study groups and discussions with peers can enhance understanding and retention.

59. Myth: CA exams have a biased marking scheme.

- Fact: ICAI ensures a standardized and fair evaluation process.

60. Myth: Older Students Can't Succeed.

- Fact: Age is just a number in CA

61. Myth: Practical Training is Unimportant.

- Fact: Practical experience is vital.

62. Myth: It's Only for Math Geniuses

- Fact:Logical thinking and hard work matter more.

63. Myth: CA is Only About Numbers

- Fact: Ethics and communication skills are crucial too.

64. Myth: Once a CA, Always Secure

- Fact: Continuous learning is essential.

These myths can create unnecessary anxiety. Stay focused, stay positive, and dispel the rumors!

CHAPTER SIXTEEN

How to Make the Most of Your Articleship /Practical Training

Articleship is a practical training program designed for aspiring Chartered Accountants (CA). It is a crucial part of the CA course, providing hands-on experience and exposure to various aspects of accounting, auditing, taxation, and financial management. Remember, the articleship period is a valuable time for learning and growth. Making the most of it will equip you with the skills and experience needed for a successful career as a Chartered Accountant.

1. Choose Wisely:

- Select a firm that offers a broad range of services and has a reputation for providing good training.

2. Be Proactive:

- Take initiative and seek out opportunities to learn and work on diverse assignments.

3. Stay Curious:

- Ask questions, seek feedback, and continuously strive to improve your knowledge and skills.

4. Document Your Work:

- Keep detailed records of the work you do, including the challenges faced and how you overcame them. This can be useful for future reference and interviews.

5. Learn from Mistakes:

- Use Mistake as learning opportunities to grow and improve.

Remember, the articleship period is a valuable time for learning and growth. Making the most of it will equip you with the skills and experience needed for a successful career as a Chartered Accountant.

CHAPTER SEVENTEEN

DUMMY ARTICLESHIPS ARE DETRIMENTAL

Dummy articleships, where students do not gain practical experience but only fulfill the requirement on paper, can be detrimental to their overall development and career prospects. Here's why:

1. Lack of Practical Experience:

- Hands-on Training: Real articleships provide invaluable hands-on experience. Students learn to apply theoretical knowledge in practical scenarios, which is crucial for understanding the nuances of accounting and auditing.

- Skill Development: Practical training helps develop essential skills such as communication, problem-solving, and time management, which are necessary for a successful career.

2. Missed Learning Opportunities:

- Exposure to Diverse Work: During articleship, students get exposed to various industries and types of work, including tax audits, statutory audits, and internal audits. This diversity is essential for building a well-rounded skill set.

- Guidance from Seniors: Working under experienced professionals provides mentorship and guidance that is invaluable for personal and professional growth.

3. Professional Networking:

- Building Contacts: Articleships offer opportunities to network with professionals, clients, and peers, which can be beneficial for future career prospects.

- Industry Insights: Interacting with industry experts and attending seminars or training sessions can provide deep insights into the profession.

4. Confidence and Competence:

- Real-world Challenges: Facing real-world challenges during articleship builds confidence and competence. It prepares students to handle complex situations in their future careers.

- Problem-Solving Skills: Practical experience helps in developing problem-solving skills, which are crucial for decision-making and leadership roles.

5. Better Job Prospects:

- Employability: Employers prefer candidates with substantial practical experience. A strong articleship background can make a significant difference during job interviews and placements.

- Professional Growth: Real articleship experience lays a solid foundation for future professional growth and opportunities.

CHAPTER EIGHTEEN

STRATEGIES FOR MANAGING STUDY TIME DURING ARTICLESHIP

1. Prioritize and Plan:

- Create a detailed study plan that aligns with your articleship schedule. Prioritize subjects and topics based on their importance and your exam timetable.

2. Use Early Mornings:

- Utilize early morning hours for studying when you are fresh and less likely to be interrupted. This can be an excellent time for focused study sessions.

3. Effective Use of Breaks:

- Make the most of breaks during your articleship workday. Use shorter breaks to review notes or solve a few practice questions.

4. Consistent Daily Study:

- Aim to study a little every day rather than cramming. Even an hour or two of focused study can add up over time and prevent last-minute stress.

5. Weekend Focus:

- Dedicate weekends or days off to longer study sessions. Use this time for in-depth study, revisions, and solving mock tests.

6. Leverage Commute Time:

- If you commute to work, use this time for lighter study tasks such as listening to recorded lectures, reviewing flashcards, or reading notes.

7. Use Technology:

- Utilize apps and online resources for studying. Digital note-taking, educational videos, and mobile apps can help you study effectively on the go.

8. Study Groups:

- Join or form a study group with fellow CA students. Group studies can help you cover more ground and understand concepts better through discussion and peer learning.

9. Focus on Weak Areas:

- Identify your weak areas and allocate more study time to them. Regularly assess your progress and adjust your study plan accordingly.

10. Stay Healthy:

- Maintain a healthy lifestyle with adequate sleep, a balanced diet, and regular exercise to keep your mind and body fit for studying.

By following a structured plan and making the most of your available time, you can effectively balance your study commitments with your articleship responsibilities. Keep pushing forward and make the most of every moment!

CHAPTER NINETEEN

ROLE OR SUPPORT OF PARENTS AND FAMILY- A LESSON FROM YOUNGEST-EVER WORLD CHESS CHAMPION.

Gukesh's rise to becoming the youngest-ever World Chess Champion at just 18 years old is nothing short of extraordinary. His journey began at the tender age of seven when he discovered his passion for chess. Recognizing his talent early on, his parents, Dr. Rajinikanth and Dr. Padma Kumari, made significant sacrifices to support his ambitions. Dr. Rajinikanth, an ENT surgeon, left his medical practice to travel with Gukesh to tournaments around the world, while Dr. Padma Kumari, a microbiologist, became the sole breadwinner for the family. Their unwavering support, financial sacrifices, and encouragement laid the foundation for Gukesh's success. Gukesh's story is a testament to the power of parental support and the impact it can have on nurturing a prodigy.

Similarly, the support from parents is crucial for CA (Chartered Accountancy) students as they navigate the rigorous and demanding journey to becoming certified professionals. The extensive study hours, financial commitments for coaching and exams, and the emotional encouragement provided by parents can make a significant difference in a student's success. Just like Gukesh, CA students thrive on the foundation of their family's unwavering support, which helps them overcome challenges and achieve their career aspirations.

Here are some key areas where family support is crucial:

Emotional Support

- Encouragement: Regularly motivate and encourage the student, especially during stressful times or setbacks.

- Understanding: Show empathy and understanding towards the pressures and challenges they face.

- Celebrating Achievements: Celebrate both small and large milestones to boost their morale and confidence.

Practical Support

- Study Environment: Help create a quiet, distraction-free study environment at home.

- Healthy Routine: Encourage a balanced routine, including proper meals, regular exercise, and adequate sleep.

- Time Management: Assist with effective time management, balancing study and relaxation periods.

Financial Support

- Course Fees: Provide financial assistance for course fees, study materials, coaching classes, and exam registrations.

- Resource Allocation: Ensure access to necessary resources like textbooks, online courses, and technological tools.

Professional Guidance

- Networking: Use family connections to introduce the student to professionals who can offer mentorship or career advice.

- Career Advice: Guide the student in making informed decisions about internships, articleship opportunities, and future career paths.

Mental and Physical Well-being

- Stress Management: Encourage practices like meditation, yoga, or hobbies to manage stress effectively.

- Health Check-ups: Ensure regular health check-ups to maintain physical well-being.

- Breaks and Relaxation: Remind the student to take regular breaks and engage in activities they enjoy.

Being Present

- Active Listening: Be available to listen to the student's concerns, fears, and aspirations.

- Family Time: Spend quality time together to maintain a strong emotional bond and provide a sense of balance.

Encouraging Independence

- Self-Reliance: Encourage the student to take responsibility for their studies and time management.

- Problem-Solving: Support the student in developing problem-solving skills and independence in their academic journey.

Communication

- Open Dialogues: Maintain open and honest communication about progress, challenges, and expectations.

- Constructive Feedback: Provide constructive feedback and avoid being overly critical or pressuring.

By offering emotional, practical, financial, and professional support, family members can significantly enhance a CA student's ability to navigate their challenging journey with confidence and determination. This holistic support system is crucial for their success and well-being.

CHAPTER TWENTY

PASS PERCENTAGE OF CA FOUNDATION, INTERMEDIATE AND FINAL EXAMS

The pass percentages for the CA Foundation, Intermediate, and Final exams have historically been relatively low, indicating the challenging nature of the course.

- **CA Foundation:**

  - Generally below 40% in recent years.
  - Highest: 44.12% (November 2018)
  - Lowest: 18.58% (June 2019)
  - September 2024: 20.47% for male candidates, 18.76% for female candidates

- **CA Intermediate:**

  - Typically in the single digits or low double digits.
  - Varies significantly between groups and attempts.
  - September 2024: 15.17% for Group 1, 15.99% for Group 2, 5.66% for both groups

- **CA Final:**

- ◦ Also generally low, often below 10%.
- ◦ Varies between groups and attempts.

  - ▪ September 2024: 9.46% for Group 1, 21.6% for Group 2, 9.42% for both groups

Key Observations:

- All three levels of the CA exams are known for their challenging nature but can be passed with right statergies
- Consistent effort, effective study strategies, and a deep understanding of the syllabus are crucial for success.
- Pass percentages can fluctuate between attempts and across different groups.

Disclaimer: This information is based on past trends and may not be indicative of future results.

For the most accurate and up-to-date information on CA pass percentages, please refer to the official website of the Institute of Chartered Accountants of India (ICAI).

Please note: These pass percentages are indicative and can vary significantly from attempt to attempt.

I hope this information is helpful!

CHAPTER TWENTY-ONE

COMMON REASONS WHY STUDENTS MAY FAIL IN CA EXAMS:

1. Lack of Proper Planning and Time Management: Many students struggle with managing their time effectively and planning their study schedule. This can lead to inadequate preparation and poor performance.

2. Insufficient Conceptual Clarity: Understanding the fundamental concepts is crucial for CA exams. Superficial knowledge or rote learning often leads to mistakes and lower scores.

3. Inadequate Study Material: Some students rely on inappropriate or insufficient study materials, ignoring the ICAI's official study materials, practice manuals, and revision test papers.

4. Poor Presentation Skills: In CA exams, presentation and clarity in answers are important. Poor presentation can result in loss of marks, even if the content is correct.

5. Lack of Practical Understanding: Theoretical knowledge alone is not enough; practical understanding and application of concepts are essential for scoring well.

6. Inadequate Revision: Many students do not allocate enough time for revision, which is crucial for retaining information and improving accuracy.

7. Distractions and Lack of Focus: Engaging in too many activities or not taking the preparation seriously can lead to distractions and reduced study time.

8. Health and Stress Management: Neglecting health, sleep, and stress management can negatively impact performance.

Addressing these issues with proper planning, focused study, and effective time management can significantly improve your chances of success in CA exams.

52

CHAPTER TWENTY-TWO

STAYING UPDATED WITH RECENT AMENDMENTS

Amendments refer to changes or updates made to laws, regulations, accounting standards, or syllabi that impact the studies and professional practices. These amendments are crucial as they ensure that the curriculum and professional guidelines stay current with evolving industry practices and legal requirements.

Staying updated with recent amendments is crucial for CA students. Here are some effective ways to keep yourself informed:

1. ICAI BoS Knowledge Portal: Regularly visit the ICAI BoS Knowledge Portal. This portal provides statutory updates, judicial updates, and other important information.

2. ICAI Official Website: Check the [ICAI Official Website](https://www.icai.org/category/announcements)regularly for announcements, notifications, and updates on exam-related amendments.

3. Email Notifications: Subscribe to ICAI's email notifications to receive updates directly in your inbox.

4. Social Media: Follow ICAI on social media platforms like Twitter, Facebook, and LinkedIn for real-time updates and announcements.

5. Study Groups and Forums: Join CA study groups and online forums where fellow students and professionals share updates and discuss recent amendments.

6. Professional Bodies and Associations: Stay connected with professional bodies and associations related to accounting and finance, as

they often share updates and resources.

By using these resources, you can ensure that you are always up-to-date with the latest amendments and changes in the CA curriculum. Good luck with your studies!

CHAPTER TWENTY-THREE

GUIDELINES ON USAGE OF CALCULATOR AND PENS AND STATIONERY IN EXAM

Calculators

Calculators are permitted in CA exams! However, there are specific guidelines you need to follow:

- Type: Only non-programmable, battery-operated, or solar-powered calculators are allowed.

- Functions: The calculator should have up to 6 functions, 12 digits, and up to two memories.

- Prohibited Features: Calculators with Bluetooth, Wi-Fi, or advanced financial functions are not allowed.

Pens and Stationery

- Pens: Only black ink pens are allowed for writing answers. Blue ink was allowed previously but is no longer permitted.

- Pencils: Pencils are allowed for drawing graphs and diagrams, but not for writing answers.

- Other Stationery: Items like erasers, sharpeners, and scales are permitted. Highlighters, markers, and correcting fluids are not allowed.

- Personal Items: You can bring a transparent water bottle, a small hand sanitizer, and your admit card.

- Borrowing/Lending: Borrowing or lending items in the exam hall is strictly prohibited.

Make sure to review the latest guidelines from the Institute of Chartered Accountants of India (ICAI) before the exam to ensure you're in compliance.

CHAPTER TWENTY-FOUR

GENERAL GUIDELINES IN EXAM

Other Guidelines regarding writing roll number, articleship number, name, religious symbols, and unfair means:

Writing Roll Number, Articleship Number, Name, and Religious Symbols

- Roll Number: You are only allowed to write your roll number in the specified place on the question paper.

- Articleship Number: Do not write your articleship number on the question paper or answer book.

- Name: Do not write your name on the question paper or answer book.

- Religious Symbols: Avoid writing any religious symbols, prayers, or distinguishing marks like Om, Swastika, 786, etc., in the answer book.

Unfair Means

ICAI takes stringent action against the adoption of unfair means during exams. Some examples of unfair means include:

- Writing on the question paper other than the roll number at the specified place.

- Writing in the answer book or additional book anything other than the roll number at the specified space.

- Possession of material inside the examination hall, such as books, notes, writing pads, or mobile phones.

- Seeking sympathy or making appeals during the exam, such as claiming a relative has passed away or requesting marks.

- Misbehaving in the exam hall or using different inks/highlighters.

Violations of these guidelines can lead to severe consequences, including the cancellation of results and debarment from future exams.

It's crucial to follow these guidelines carefully to avoid any issues during the exam.

Make sure to review the latest guidelines from the Institute of Chartered Accountants of India (ICAI) before the exam to ensure you're in compliance.

CHAPTER TWENTY-FIVE

GUIDELINES ON UNDERLINING IN EXAM

Underlining is allowed in your CA exams. However, it is essential to use this technique judiciously and follow specific guidelines to ensure your answer script is neat and complies with ICAI's standards:

Guidelines for Underlining

- Purposeful Underlining: Use underlining to highlight key points, headings, or important sections of your answers.

- Consistency: Be consistent with your underlining style. Use a single, straight line for underlining, and avoid making your answer script appear cluttered.

- Approved Pen: Use only the permitted black ink pen for underlining, as other colors or highlighters are not allowed.

Make sure to review the latest guidelines from the Institute of Chartered Accountants of India (ICAI) before the exam to ensure you're in compliance.

General Tips for Answer Presentation

- Neatness: Keep your handwriting neat and legible.

- Margins: Use margins for making notes or additional points, but avoid crowding the answer space.

- Numbering: Number your answers clearly as per the question paper.

- Structured Answers: Write structured answers with headings, subheadings, and bullet points where necessary to enhance readability.

Following these guidelines will ensure your answer script is well-presented and highlights the essential points effectively.

Make sure to review the latest guidelines from the Institute of Chartered Accountants of India (ICAI) before the exam to ensure you're in compliance.

CHAPTER TWENTY-SIX

ESSENTIAL STATIONARY DURING PREPARATION FOR CA EXAM

Having the right stationery can make your CA study sessions more efficient and organized. Here's a list of essential stationery items for CA students:

1. Writing Instruments

- Pens: Black ink pens (since they are required for exams) and a few blue ink pens for practice.

- Pencils: Mechanical or regular pencils for diagrams and rough work.

- Erasers and Sharpeners: Necessary for corrections and sharpening pencils.

2. Note-taking Supplies

- Notebooks: Several notebooks for different subjects to keep your notes organized.

- Sticky Notes: For jotting down quick reminders or important points.

- Highlighters: To emphasize key points in your notes and textbooks.

- Index Cards: Useful for making flashcards for quick revision.

3. Organizational Tools

- Files and Folders: To organize loose sheets, assignments, and important documents.

- Binders: For holding printed study materials and notes.

- Dividers: To categorize sections within binders or notebooks.

4. Measurement Tools

- Ruler/Scale: For drawing lines, graphs, and diagrams.

- Protractor and Compass: Useful for geometry and drawing accurate shapes.

5. Calculation Aids

- Non-programmable Calculator: Essential for practicing calculations and allowed in exams.

- Logarithm Table and Financial Calculator: For complex calculations (if applicable).

6. Study Aids

- Bookmarks: To mark important pages in textbooks or notebooks.

- Desk Planner or Calendar: For scheduling study sessions and keeping track of important dates.

- Sticky Flags: For marking specific sections in textbooks or notes.

7. Digital Tools

- Laptop/Tablet: For accessing digital study materials, online courses, and practice tests.

- USB Drive or External Hard Drive: For backing up important files and documents.

8. Miscellaneous

- Whiteboard and Markers: For visual learning and practicing problems.

- Desk Lamp: To ensure proper lighting during study sessions.

- Paper Clips and Staplers: To keep papers together and organized.

Having these essential stationery items will help you stay organized, efficient, and focused during your CA studies. Good luck with your preparation!

CHAPTER TWENTY-SEVEN

Useful Gadgets during CA Journey

Equipping yourself with the right gadgets can significantly enhance your preparation for the CA exam. Here are some essential gadgets that can aid in your study process:

1. Laptop or Desktop Computer

- Uses: Access online study materials, attend virtual classes, take mock tests, and organize notes.

- Features to Look For: Reliable performance, good battery life, and sufficient storage.

2. Tablet or E-Reader

- Uses: Portable access to e-books, PDFs, and other study materials. Great for reading on the go.

- Features to Look For: Lightweight, good display quality, and long battery life.

3. Smartphone

- Uses: Educational apps, quick access to online resources, and communication with peers and mentors.

- Features to Look For: Good performance, reliable internet connectivity, and sufficient storage.

4. Noise-Cancelling Headphones

- Uses: Minimize distractions while studying, especially useful during online classes and self-study sessions.

- Features to Look For: Effective noise cancellation, comfortable fit, and long battery life.

5. External Hard Drive or USB Drive

- Uses: Backup important files and study materials to avoid data loss.

- Features to Look For: High storage capacity, portability, and reliable performance.

6. Printer and Scanner (if possible)

- Uses: Print out study materials, practice papers, and scan important documents.

- Features to Look For: Multi-function (print, scan, copy), reliable performance, and cost-effectiveness.

7. Smartwatch or Fitness Tracker

- Uses: Monitor your health, manage study breaks, and set reminders.

- Features to Look For: Health tracking features, long battery life, and synchronization with your smartphone.

8. External Monitor(if possible)

- Uses: Extended screen space for multitasking, especially useful for comparing notes and practice questions.

- Features to Look For: Good display quality, adjustable stand, and appropriate size.

9. Webcam and Microphone

- Uses: Participate in virtual classes and discussions with clarity.

- Features to Look For: High-resolution camera and clear audio quality.

10. Power Bank

- Uses: Ensure your devices stay charged during long study sessions, especially when on the go.

- Features to Look For: High capacity, fast charging, and portability.

11. Ergonomic Accessories(very much Important)

- Uses: Maintain good posture and comfort during long study hours.

- Features to Look For: Ergonomic chair, adjustable desk, wrist rest, and monitor stand.

Having these gadgets can enhance your efficiency, comfort, and productivity during your CA exam preparation. Investing in the right tools can make a significant difference in your study experience.

CHAPTER TWENTY-EIGHT

EFFECTIVE STUDY AND MEMORY TECHNIQUES - THE OLYMPICS SECRET

The story of the British cycling team's success at the Olympics is truly inspiring and a testament to the power of strategic planning and perseverance. Here's a brief overview:

The Transformation

In 2002, Sir Dave Brailsford was appointed as the Performance Director of British Cycling. At the time, British cycling had a poor track record, with only one gold medal in its 76-year history. Brailsford introduced a philosophy called "the aggregation of marginal gains", which focused on making small improvements in everything they did.

Marginal Gains

Brailsford and his team made numerous small changes that collectively had a significant impact. They redesigned bike seats, used alcohol on tires for better grip, and even painted the team truck white to spot dust particles. These tiny improvements added up to create a more efficient and competitive team.

Olympic Success

The results were remarkable. At the 2008 Beijing Olympics, the British cycling team won seven out of ten gold medals available in track cycling. They repeated this success at the 2012 London Olympics, winning multiple gold medals and setting new records. The team continued to dominate in subsequent Olympics, including the 2016 Rio Olympics and beyond.

Legacy

The success of the British cycling team has not only brought glory to the nation but also inspired other sports teams to adopt similar strategies. The team's achievements are a testament to the power of dedication, innovation, and the belief that small changes can lead to big results.

Imagine the British cycling team as a group of CA students facing their exams. Back in 2002, their performance was dismal – much like struggling with tough subjects and low confidence. Enter Sir Dave Brailsford, their new mentor, who introduced the concept of "marginal gains" – improving everything by just 1% everyday.

Marginal Gains for CA Students

Brailsford focused on tiny changes: redesigning bike seats, using better tires, and even painting the truck white to spot dust. Similarly, as CA students, you can:

- Optimize Study Environment: Keep your study space clean and organized.

- Enhance Study Techniques: Use mind maps, flashcards, and summaries.

- Health & Well-being: Maintain a balanced diet, regular exercise, and adequate sleep.

Consistency and Persistence

The British team practiced consistently and made small daily improvements. For CA students, this means:

- Daily Practice: Set aside time each day for consistent study.

- Regular Reviews: Continuously review and refine your study methods.

Achieving Greatness

Just as the British cycling team won seven gold medals at the 2008 Beijing Olympics, by applying these principles, CA students can achieve excellence. Their journey shows that small, consistent efforts lead to significant results.

Key Takeaways

- Small Improvements Matter: Focus on marginal gains in every aspect of your study routine.

- Consistency is Key: Regular, persistent effort beats sporadic, intense studying.

- Holistic Approach: Balance academics with health and well-being.

By adopting the mindset of the British cycling team, you can pedal your way to success in your CA exams. 🚴‍♂️

Go ahead, start applying those small improvements today!

EXPLORING ANCIENT STUDY TECHNIQUES

Exploring ancient study techniques can provide valuable insights and strategies that can still be beneficial for CA students today. Here are some ancient techniques that have stood the test of time and can be adapted to modern study practices:

1. The Socratic Method

Origin: Ancient Greece, attributed to Socrates

Description:

- Questioning Approach: Engage in a dialogue where you ask and answer questions to stimulate critical thinking and illuminate ideas.

- Application for CA Students: Use this method to deeply understand accounting principles and concepts. Formulate questions on each topic and answer them to ensure thorough comprehension.

2. The Trivium

Origin: Ancient Rome

Description:

- Grammar: Focus on understanding the fundamental principles and rules.

- Logic: Develop reasoning and critical thinking skills.

- Rhetoric: Learn to communicate ideas effectively.

- Application for CA Students: Apply the trivium to study CA subjects: start with understanding the basics (grammar), analyze and reason through problems (logic), and explain concepts clearly (rhetoric).

3. Memory Palaces (Method of Loci)

Origin: Ancient Greece and Rome, used by orators like Cicero

Description:

- Visualization Technique: Create a mental image of a familiar place (palace) and associate each piece of information with a specific location within this place.

- Application for CA Students: Use this technique to memorize accounting standards, formulas, or key concepts by placing them in different rooms of your memory palace.

4. Meditation and Mindfulness

Origin: Ancient India, practiced in various forms of yoga and Buddhism

Description:

- Mental Clarity and Focus: Regular practice of meditation and mindfulness can help improve concentration and reduce stress.

- Application for CA Students: Incorporate mindfulness exercises or meditation into your daily routine to enhance focus and manage exam stress effectively.

5. Teach Back Method

Origin: Ancient Egypt, used by scholars and scribes

Description:

- Learning Through Teaching: Teach the material you have learned to someone else, which reinforces your own understanding.

- Application for CA Students: Explain accounting concepts and principles to peers or even to yourself. This technique ensures you understand the material deeply.

6. Copying and Repetition

Origin: Ancient China, practiced by Confucian scholars

Description:

- Writing Practice: Repeatedly copying important texts to reinforce memory and understanding.

- Application for CA Students: Write out important formulas, definitions, and principles multiple times. Repetition can help with memorization and retention.

By adapting these ancient techniques to your modern study practices, you can enhance your learning experience and improve your retention and understanding of complex CA subjects. Embrace the wisdom of the past to succeed in the present!

CHAPTER THIRTY

ACTIVE LEARNING METHODS

The CA exam demands deep understanding and retention of complex concepts. Here are some active study techniques that can significantly enhance your learning and boost your chances of success:

1. **Concept Mapping:**

   - **Visualize Relationships:** Create mind maps or concept maps to visually connect different topics and subtopics. This helps in understanding the bigger picture and identifying relationships between concepts.
   - **Example:** For accounting standards, create a mind map connecting the standard number, its objectives, scope, and key requirements.

2. **Teach or Explain Concepts:**

   - **Reinforce Understanding:** Explain concepts to yourself or someone else. This forces you to articulate your understanding and identify any gaps in your knowledge.
   - **Consider a Study Group:** Teaching concepts to peers can be mutually beneficial and provide diverse perspectives.

3. **Practice with Past Papers and Mock Tests:**

   - **Simulate Exam Conditions:** Solve past exam papers and mock tests under timed conditions to get accustomed to the exam format and improve time management skills.

- **Identify Weak Areas:** Analyze your performance in mock tests to identify areas of weakness and focus your revision efforts accordingly.

4. **Spaced Repetition:**

- **Review at Increasing Intervals:** Review previously studied material at increasing intervals (e.g., day 1, day 3, day 7, day 14). This technique helps in long-term retention and reinforces learning.

5. **Use Flashcards:**

- **Memorize Key Concepts:** Create flashcards for key definitions, formulas, and important points. Regularly review these flashcards to reinforce memory and quick recall.

6. **Mind Palace Technique:**

- **Visualize and Associate:** Create a mental palace (a familiar place) and associate different concepts with specific locations within that palace. This technique can help with memorization and recall.

7. **Stay Updated with Current Developments:**

- **Follow Industry Trends:** Stay updated with the latest industry news, accounting standards, and amendments through professional journals, online resources, and ICAI publications.

1. **Maintain a Healthy Lifestyle:**

- **Prioritize Well-being:** Ensure adequate sleep, exercise, and a balanced diet. A healthy mind and body are essential for effective learning and stress management.

Additional Tips:

- **Create a Study Schedule:** A well-structured study schedule helps in maintaining consistency and maximizing your study time.
- **Break Down Large Topics:** Divide large topics into smaller, more manageable chunks.
- **Take Regular Breaks:** Short breaks during study sessions can help maintain focus and prevent burnout.
- **Seek Clarification:** Don't hesitate to seek clarification from faculty, mentors, or fellow students if you have any doubts or questions.

By incorporating these active study techniques into your preparation, you can enhance your understanding, improve retention, and increase your chances of success in the challenging CA exams.

Disclaimer: The effectiveness of these techniques may vary depending on individual learning styles and preferences. Experiment with different techniques to find what works best for you.

CHAPTER THIRTY-ONE

WRITING - A POWERFUL TOOL FOR MEMORY AND MANIFESTATION

Writing is a powerful tool for enhancing memory and manifesting goals, especially in the rigorous journey of becoming a Chartered Accountant (CA). Here's how writing can significantly aid CA students:

1. Enhancing Memory Retention

- Active Engagement: Writing involves active engagement with the material. When you write, you process information more deeply, which helps in better retention.

- Summarization: Creating summaries of complex topics helps in consolidating your understanding and making information easier to recall.

- Repetition: Regularly writing and rewriting key concepts reinforces them in your memory.

2. Clarifying Thoughts and Concepts

- Organized Thinking: Writing helps in organizing your thoughts logically. It enables you to break down complex topics into simpler, digestible parts.

- Conceptual Clarity: Putting thoughts into words forces you to articulate and clarify your understanding, leading to deeper insights.

3. Goal Setting and Manifestation

- Written Goals: Writing down your goals makes them tangible and concrete. It provides a clear roadmap for your CA journey.

- Commitment: The act of writing your goals is a commitment to yourself. It signals to your subconscious mind that these goals are important.

- Visualization: Describing your goals in detail helps in visualizing success, which can boost confidence and motivation.

4. Effective Study Techniques

- Note-Taking: Taking detailed notes during classes or self-study sessions helps in capturing essential information for later review.

- Mind Mapping: Creating visual representations of topics through mind maps aids in understanding relationships between different concepts.

- Practice Writing: Regularly writing out practice answers for potential exam questions improves your ability to recall and articulate information during exams.

5. Stress Reduction

- Journaling: Keeping a study journal can be a great way to manage stress. Writing about your challenges, progress, and emotions can provide relief and keep you focused.

- Reflective Writing: Reflecting on your study sessions and identifying areas of improvement can enhance your learning experience.

6. Continuous Improvement

- Feedback Loop: Reviewing your written work and seeking feedback helps in identifying mistakes and areas for improvement.

- Self-Assessment: Writing helps in self-assessment by allowing you to track your progress and adjust your study strategies accordingly.

Practical Tips for Using Writing Effectively

1. Daily Writing Habit: Develop a habit of writing daily, whether it's notes, summaries, or reflections.

2. Structured Notes: Keep your notes structured with headings, subheadings, and bullet points for better organization.

3. Review Regularly: Regularly review and revise your written notes to reinforce memory.

4. Goal Journal: Maintain a journal where you write down your goals, action plans, and progress.

5. Mind Maps and Diagrams: Use mind maps and diagrams to visualize and connect different concepts.

By incorporating writing into your study routine, you can enhance your memory, gain clarity, and stay committed to your goals. Writing transforms abstract ideas into tangible actions, making it a powerful tool for success in the CA journey.

CHAPTER THIRTY-TWO

EFFECTIVE NOTE-TAKING STRATEGIES

Effective note-taking is crucial for CA students, given the vast amount of information they need to absorb and recall. Here are some proven note-taking strategies tailored for CA students:

1. The Cornell Method

- Structure: Divide your page into three sections: a narrow column on the left for cues, a wider column on the right for notes, and a summary section at the bottom.

- Cues: Use the left column to write down keywords, questions, or main ideas.

- Notes: In the right column, jot down detailed notes during lectures or while studying.

- Summary: After the session, write a brief summary of the notes in the bottom section to reinforce your understanding.

2. Mind Mapping

- Visual Learning: Create a mind map with the main topic at the center and branches for subtopics and key points.

- Connections: Use lines to connect related ideas, helping you see the relationships between different concepts.

- Color Coding: Use different colors for different branches or sections to make the map more visually engaging.

3. The Outline Method

- Hierarchy: Structure your notes in an organized, hierarchical format with headings, subheadings, and bullet points.

- Clarity: This method helps in maintaining a clear structure and is useful for subjects with a lot of detailed information.

- Consistency: Keep a consistent format to easily track and review the notes.

4. Charting Method

- Columns: Create a table or chart with columns for different categories or topics.

- Comparison: This method is particularly useful for comparing and contrasting similar concepts or data sets.

- Quick Reference: Helps in quickly locating specific information for review.

5. Sentence Method

- Detail-Oriented: Write every new thought or idea on a separate line, using sentences or short phrases.

- Flexibility: Offers flexibility in recording information as it flows during lectures or reading sessions.

- Review: This method can be helpful for reviewing detailed explanations and examples.

6. Digital Note-Taking

- Apps and Tools: Use digital tools like OneNote, Evernote, or Notion to take and organize notes.

- Searchability: Digital notes are easily searchable, allowing you to quickly find specific information.

- Multimedia: Include multimedia elements like images, links, and recordings to enhance your notes.

7. Highlighting and Annotating

- Key Points: Highlight or underline key points in your notes or textbooks.

- Annotations: Add brief notes or comments in the margins to clarify or emphasize important concepts.

- Color Coding: Use different colors to highlight different types of information, such as definitions, formulas, and examples.

8. Concept Mapping

- Relationships: Create diagrams that show relationships between concepts, similar to mind maps but more focused on connections and flows.

- Detailed Links: Include arrows, labels, and notes to explain how different concepts are related.

9. Flashcards

- Quick Recall: Write down questions on one side and answers on the other. Regularly quiz yourself to reinforce memory.

- Portable: Flashcards are portable and can be reviewed anywhere, making them perfect for quick study sessions.

10. Combination Method

- Integrated Approach: Combine different methods based on the subject matter and your personal preference. For example, use the Cornell Method for lectures, mind mapping for complex topics, and flashcards for quick revision.

Tips for Effective Note-Taking

1. Active Listening: Pay close attention during lectures or study sessions to identify key points.

2. Summarize: Write notes in your own words to ensure you understand the material.

3. Review and Revise: Regularly review and revise your notes to reinforce learning and make necessary updates.

4. Stay Organized: Keep your notes well-organized and categorized by subject and topic.

By incorporating these note-taking strategies, you can enhance your learning efficiency, improve retention, and make your study sessions more productive. Happy studying!

CHAPTER THIRTY-THREE

SPEED READING TECHNIQUES

Speed reading can be a valuable skill for CA students to efficiently process large volumes of study material. Here are some effective speed reading techniques tailored for CA students:

1. Preview the Material:

- Scan the Text: Before diving deep, quickly scan the headings, subheadings, and any highlighted or bold text to get an overview of the material.

- Identify Key Points: Note any key points or concepts that you need to pay special attention to.

2. Avoid Subvocalization:

- Silent Reading: Try to avoid reading out loud in your mind (subvocalization). Instead, focus on seeing the words and understanding their meaning.

- Guide Your Eyes: Use a pointer, like your finger or a pen, to guide your eyes along the lines. This can help in reducing subvocalization and increasing reading speed.

3. Practice Chunking:

- Read in Chunks: Instead of reading word by word, practice reading groups of words or phrases. This helps in processing information faster.

- Expand Your Vision: Train your eyes to take in more words at a glance by practicing with wider chunks of text.

4. Use Peripheral Vision:

- Widen Your Focus: Use your peripheral vision to read more words in a single glance. Practice focusing on the middle of a line while taking in the words on the sides.

- Vertical Reading: Try reading down the page vertically, rather than left to right, to take in more information at once.

5. Skim and Scan:

- Skim for Main Ideas: Quickly move your eyes over the text to get the gist of the content. Focus on main ideas and keywords.

- Scan for Specific Information: Look for specific information by scanning the text quickly rather than reading every word.

6. Improve Comprehension:

- Summarize as You Go: Periodically stop and summarize what you've read in your own words. This helps in retaining and understanding the information.

- Ask Questions: Ask yourself questions about the material and look for answers as you read. This keeps you engaged and improves comprehension.

7. Regular Practice:

- Daily Reading: Dedicate time each day to practice speed reading with various texts. Start with easier material and gradually move to more complex content.

- Use Speed Reading Apps: Consider using speed reading apps or tools that can help track your progress and provide structured practice.

Example Practice Session:

Warm-Up (5 minutes):

- Preview: Scan the table of contents or headings.

- Identify: Note any key terms or concepts.

Reading Session (20 minutes):

- Speed Reading Techniques: Apply chunking and peripheral vision.

- Skim and Scan: Focus on main ideas and keywords.

Review (5 minutes):

- Summarize: Write down or mentally summarize key points.

- Questions: Reflect on any questions and look for answers in the material.

By incorporating these techniques and dedicating regular time to practice, you can significantly improve your reading speed and efficiency, making it easier to handle the extensive CA study material. Happy reading!

CHAPTER THIRTY-FOUR

FINGERING TECHNIQUE

The "fingering technique" for study, particularly for CA students, refers to a method of actively engaging with physical study materials using your fingers. This approach can enhance concentration and memory retention. Here are some ways to apply this technique effectively:

1. Reading with Finger Tracing

- Enhanced Focus: Use your finger to trace the lines as you read. This keeps your eyes and mind focused on the text, reducing distractions.

- Better Retention: Physically engaging with the text helps in better retention of information.

2. Highlighting and Underlining

- Active Participation: Use your fingers to hold a highlighter or pen and underline key points as you read. This makes you an active participant in the learning process.

- Emphasis on Important Information: Highlighting important information helps in quickly identifying key concepts during revision.

3. Note-Taking and Annotation

- Handwritten Notes: Use your fingers to write notes by hand. Handwriting activates different parts of the brain compared to typing, aiding memory retention.

- Annotations: Make annotations in the margins of your textbooks or notes using your fingers. This helps in summarizing and clarifying concepts.

4. Flashcards and Index Cards

- Interactive Learning: Create flashcards with key concepts and use your fingers to flip through them. This tactile engagement helps in reinforcing memory.

- Quick Reviews: Use your fingers to shuffle and organize flashcards for quick review sessions.

5. Drawing Diagrams and Mind Maps

- Visual Representation: Draw diagrams, charts, and mind maps using your fingers. This visual representation helps in understanding and recalling complex concepts.

- Connections: Physically drawing connections between ideas helps in seeing the relationships between different topics.

6. Practical Problem Solving

- Step-by-Step Solutions: Use your fingers to write out step-by-step solutions to problems. This methodical approach ensures thorough understanding.

- Repetition: Regular practice with your fingers enhances muscle memory and speed in solving problems.

7. Organizing Study Materials

- Manual Sorting: Use your fingers to sort and organize study materials, such as notes, flashcards, and textbooks. Keeping everything in order helps in efficient study sessions.

- Tactile Interaction: Physically interacting with your study materials can enhance your engagement and connection with the content.

Tips for Effective Use of Fingering Technique

1. Comfortable Workspace: Ensure you have a comfortable and well-organized study space.

2. Quality Stationery: Use quality pens, highlighters, and paper that you enjoy using.

3. Regular Breaks: Take regular breaks to avoid strain and keep your mind fresh.

4. Consistency: Incorporate the fingering technique into your daily study routine for consistent results.

By incorporating the fingering technique into your study routine, you can enhance your focus, retention, and overall learning experience. This hands-on approach engages multiple senses, making your study sessions more productive and effective.

MEMORY TECHNIQUES FOR CA STUDENTS

For CA (Chartered Accountancy) students, effective memory techniques can make a significant difference in retaining complex information. Here are a few tried-and-tested methods to help you out:

1. Mnemonics:

- Create acronyms or short phrases to remember lists or key points. For example, to recall the accounting principles, you can use the acronym "ABCDE" for Accuracy, Balance, Consistency, Documentation, and Ethical standards.

2. Visualization:

- Turn information into vivid, memorable images in your mind. For instance, imagine a balance scale when thinking of balance sheets.

3. Mind Mapping:

- Use mind maps to visually organize information. Start with a central concept and branch out into related subtopics. This technique helps in connecting different pieces of information and seeing the bigger picture.

4. Chunking:

- Break down large amounts of information into smaller, manageable chunks. For example, divide a long accounting standard into sections and tackle them one at a time.

5. Spaced Repetition:

- Revisit the material at spaced intervals. This method helps move information from short-term to long-term memory.

6. Teach Someone Else:

- Explaining concepts to someone else is a great way to reinforce your understanding and memory. If you can teach it, you understand it.

7. Flashcards:

- Create flashcards for important terms, definitions, and formulas. Regularly review them to reinforce your memory.

8. Association:

- Link new information to something you already know. Associating a new concept with a familiar one makes it easier to remember.

9. Practice Questions:

- Regularly solve practice questions and past papers. This not only helps with retention but also familiarizes you with the exam format.

10. Healthy Lifestyle:

- Maintain a healthy diet, get regular exercise, and ensure adequate sleep. A healthy body supports a sharp mind.

Example Mnemonic for Financial Ratios:

To remember liquidity ratios:

- Current Ratio: "Current assets over Current liabilities."

- Quick Ratio: "Quick assets over Current liabilities" (Quick assets = Current assets - Inventory).

Visual Aid:

```

[Current Assets]

-----------------

[Current Liabilities]

```

Use these techniques consistently, and you'll find your memory and understanding of complex CA subjects improving significantly. Happy studying! ??

CHAPTER THIRTY-SIX

MEMORY PALACE TECHNIQUE FOR CA STUDENTS

The Memory Palace technique, also known as the Method of Loci, is a powerful mnemonic strategy that can help CA students retain and recall complex information. Here's a step-by-step guide to using this technique effectively:

Memory Palace Technique for CA Students

1. Choose Your Palace:

- Select a familiar place, such as your home, a route you take daily, or even a favorite fictional location. The more familiar you are with the place, the better.

2. Define Key Points:

- Identify the key concepts or items you need to remember. For example, important accounting standards, formulas, financial ratios, or steps in a process.

3. Create Distinct Locations:

- Assign each key point to a specific location within your chosen palace. For instance, you could place one concept in your living room, another in the kitchen, and another in your bedroom.

4. Visualize and Associate:

- Visualize walking through your palace, placing each key point in its designated spot. Create vivid, memorable images for each concept. The more unusual or exaggerated the image, the better it will stick in your mind.

- Example: To remember the accounting principle of "Consistency," imagine a rigid statue of an accountant consistently polishing a golden balance sheet in your kitchen.

5. Link Information:

- Connect additional details or sub-points to the main image in each location. This helps create a rich, multi-layered memory.

- Example: For "Consistency," you could add the statue holding a list of consistent accounting practices, like always using the same inventory valuation method.

6. Practice the Journey:

- Mentally walk through your Memory Palace regularly, reinforcing the associations and making sure you remember each key point and its details.

7. Use Multiple Palaces:

- If you have a lot of information to remember, create multiple Memory Palaces. For example, one for accounting principles, another for financial ratios, and another for tax regulations.

8. Review and Update:

- Periodically review your Memory Palace to ensure the information stays fresh. Update it as needed with new information.

Example Memory Palace Walkthrough:

Palace: Your Home

- Living Room:
- Key Point: Accounting Principle of Consistency
- Image: A statue of an accountant polishing a golden balance sheet.
- Kitchen:
- Key Point: Matching Principle
- Image: A chef matching ingredients to recipes while balancing a ledger.
- Bedroom:
- Key Point: Revenue Recognition Principle
- Image: A calendar with dollar bills flying out of it, signifying revenue being recorded.

How to Visualize:

Imagine walking through your home. As you enter the living room, you see the statue of the accountant, reminding you of the principle of consistency. Moving to the kitchen, you see the chef balancing ingredients and a ledger, reminding you of the matching principle. Finally, in the bedroom, the calendar with flying dollar bills reminds you of the revenue recognition principle.

By using these vivid, imaginative associations, you can make abstract concepts more concrete and easier to recall during your exams.

Happy memorizing! ???

MEMORY PALACE TECHNIQUE WITH RELATIVES INSTEAD OF PLACES

Using the memory palace technique with relatives instead of places can be a creative and effective way to remember information. Let's walk through the steps:

Steps to Create a Memory Palace Using Relatives

1. Select Relatives

Choose a set of relatives that you know well and can easily visualize. Each relative will represent a different piece of information.

2. Assign Information to Relatives

Link specific pieces of information to each relative. Use their unique characteristics, habits, or traits to make the associations more vivid and memorable.

3. Create Visual and Interactive Stories

Imagine your relatives interacting with the information in a memorable way. The more detailed and imaginative the visualization, the better.

Example: Memorizing Accounting Principles

Relatives as Memory Points:

1. Grandfather: Represents the basic accounting equation.

2. Grandmother: Represents the principles of revenue recognition.

3. Father: Represents the matching principle.

4. Mother: Represents the principle of materiality.

5. Brother: Represents the principle of prudence.

6. Sister: Represents the principle of consistency.

Visual and Interactive Stories:

1. Grandfather (Accounting Equation)

- Visualize your grandfather holding a giant scale with "Assets" on one side and "Liabilities + Equity" on the other, balancing them perfectly.

2. Grandmother (Revenue Recognition)

- Imagine your grandmother baking a cake. She only considers the cake "sold" once the entire recipe (transaction) is completed and the cake is handed over to the customer.

3. Father (Matching Principle)

- Picture your father working in his garden. For every seed he plants (expense), he notes down when the flowers bloom (revenue), ensuring each expense is matched with its corresponding revenue.

4. Mother (Materiality Principle)

- See your mother organizing her pantry. She keeps only significant and important items in the front, representing material items that should be clearly reported in financial statements.

5. Brother (Prudence Principle)

- Imagine your brother wearing safety gear while riding his bike. He represents the prudence principle by always preparing for potential risks and uncertainties.

6. Sister (Consistency Principle)

- Visualize your sister painting a wall. She uses the same brush and paint type each time, symbolizing the principle of consistency in applying accounting methods.

Tips for Effective Visualization

- Be Creative: Use vivid and imaginative stories that make the information memorable.

- Include Emotions: Add emotions or funny elements to make the stories more engaging.

- Regular Review: Walk through your memory palace regularly to reinforce the connections.

By using relatives in your memory palace, you can create strong associations that make it easier to recall complex information. This technique leverages your familiarity with your relatives to anchor and organize your memory.

Ready to build your memory palace with your family?

TIPS TO REMEMBER THE NUMBERS

Remembering numbers can be quite challenging, but there are several effective memory techniques that can help. Here are a few methods you can use:

1. Mnemonic Devices

Create a story or phrase where each word starts with the same letter as the number you need to remember. For example, for the number 12345:

- Story: "One sunny day, two kids had three ice creams, four balloons, and five smiles."

- This story can make the number more memorable by associating it with a vivid image or narrative.

2. Chunking

Break down the number into smaller, manageable chunks. Our brains find it easier to remember shorter sequences.

- Example: Instead of trying to remember 9876543210 as a single string, break it down into chunks: 987-654-3210.

3. The Major System

Convert numbers into consonant sounds, then form words with those consonants. This technique is particularly useful for long numbers.

- System:

- 0 = s, z

- 1 = t, d

- 2 = n

- 3 = m

- 4 = r

- 5 = l

- 6 = j, sh, ch
- 7 = k, g
- 8 = f, v
- 9 = p, b
- Example: To remember the number 345, you might convert it to "M R L," and then create a memorable phrase like "Merry Lion."

4. Visualization

Transform numbers into visual images or objects that you can mentally picture.

- Example: To remember the number 123, imagine a single (1) tree (2) with three (3) apples hanging from it.

5. The Peg System

Create a list of words or objects (pegs) associated with numbers, then create mental images to link the items you need to remember with these pegs.

- Example Pegs: 1 = sun, 2 = shoe, 3 = tree, 4 = door, 5 = hive, etc.
- To remember the number 245: Picture a shoe (2) with a hive (5) near a door (4).

6. The Memory Palace Technique

Use a familiar place and mentally "place" numbers at different locations within this place.

- Example: Imagine your home and place the number 123 at the front door, 456 in the living room, 789 in the kitchen. When you need to recall the numbers, visualize walking through your house and picking them up.

Practical Example for CA Students

Let's use the chunking method for remembering the following critical figures:

- Number: 567398214
- Chunked: 567-398-214

You could create a story with these chunks:

- Imagine that there are 567 (five hundred sixty-seven) students in a conference.
- They have 398 (three hundred ninety-eight) pages of notes.
- They attend 214 (two hundred fourteen) sessions.

Tips for Practicing These Techniques

1. Regular Practice: Practice these techniques regularly to improve your ability to remember numbers.

2. Use Real-Life Examples: Apply these methods to real-life numbers you need to remember, such as phone numbers, dates, or financial figures.

3. Stay Consistent: Consistency is key. Choose a technique that works best for you and stick with it.

By using these memory techniques, you can enhance your ability to remember numbers effectively and make your study sessions more productive. ??

Which technique do you think will work best for you?

CHAPTER THIRTY-NINE

TIPS TO REMEMBER THE NUMBERS AND THE CORRESPONDING LETTERS IN THE MAJOR SYSTEM OF MEMORY

To remember the numbers and the corresponding letters in the Major System of memory, you can use mnemonic techniques and visual associations. Here's a way to do it:

Major System Overview

Each number from 0 to 9 is associated with specific consonant sounds. Here is the basic system:

Number	Consonant(s)
0	s, z
1	t, d
2	n
3	m
4	r
5	l
6	j, sh, ch
7	k, g
8	f, v
9	p, b

Mnemonic Techniques and Visual Associations

0 - s, z

- Mnemonic: Zero

- Visual: Picture a zero (0) shaped like a snake (s).

1 - t, d

- Mnemonic: Tall (1 looks like a tall stick)

- Visual: Imagine the number 1 as a tall tree (t).

2 - n

- Mnemonic: Two (2) has two down strokes, like the shape of "n."

- Visual: Picture the number 2 looking like a swan (n).

3 - m

- Mnemonic: Three (3) has three humps if you draw an "m".

- Visual: Visualize the number 3 as three mountains (m).

4 - r

- Mnemonic: Four (4) ends with an "r."

- Visual: Imagine a number 4 with a runner (r) racing.

5 - l

- Mnemonic: Five (5) resembles an outstretched hand with all five fingers (l).

- Visual: Picture the number 5 as an outstretched palm (l).

6 - j, sh, ch

- Mnemonic: Six (6) looks like a hook, like the "j" shape.

- Visual: Visualize the number 6 as a fishing hook (j).

7 - k, g

- Mnemonic: Seven (7) looks like a sideways "K."

- Visual: Imagine the number 7 as a boomerang (k).

8 - f, v

- Mnemonic: Eight (8) looks like a pair of spectacles, with two loops like an "f."

- Visual: Picture the number 8 as a pair of spectacles (f).

9 - p, b

- Mnemonic: Nine (9) looks like a balloon with a string, similar to the shape of "p" and "b."

- Visual: Visualize the number 9 as a balloon (p).

Example Word Association

To remember the number 23, you can form the word "name":

- 2 (n)

- 3 (m)

By creating visual and mnemonic associations, you can effectively remember the numbers and their corresponding letters in the Major System. Practice regularly, and soon it will become second nature! ??

95

CHAPTER FORTY

TECHNIQUES FOR REMEMBERING SECTION NUMBERS IN LAW

Remembering section numbers for CA students can be challenging due to the vast amount of information. However, using effective memorization techniques can make it easier. Here are some strategies:

Techniques for Remembering Section Numbers

1. Mnemonics:

- Create mnemonic devices to associate section numbers with specific keywords or concepts. For example, for Section 194J of the Income Tax Act (TDS on Professional Fees), you can create a mnemonic like "Jolly Professionals."

2. Visualization:

- Visualize the section number as part of a story or image related to the concept. For instance, imagine a scenario where "Section 80C" is linked to saving for investments in a piggy bank.

3. Mind Maps:

- Use mind maps to visually organize and connect different sections. This technique helps in visualizing the relationships between sections and concepts, making them easier to recall.

4. Flashcards:

- Create flashcards with the section number on one side and the details on the other. Regularly review these flashcards to reinforce your memory.

5. Chunking:

- Break down the information into smaller, manageable chunks. Group similar sections together and study them as a set. This makes it easier to remember related sections.

6. Repetition:

- Regularly review and repeat the section numbers and their details. Spaced repetition techniques, such as using apps like Anki, can help reinforce your memory over time.

7. Teach Back Method:

- Teach the sections and their details to someone else. Teaching reinforces your understanding and helps in retaining the information.

8. Association Techniques:

- Associate section numbers with familiar things or events. For example, if Section 269SS (related to accepting loans in certain modes) reminds you of a birthday on June 9th (6/9), you can link the section number to that date.

Example Mnemonic and Visualization

Mnemonic:

- Section 80C: "80 Cookies" (relate cookies to savings and investments, as it covers deductions for investments).

Visualization:

- Section 194J: Imagine a joyful professional in a courtroom, linking "J" with "Jolly Professional" to remember TDS on Professional Fees.

Flashcard

Here's a simple text-based structure to illustrate:

Flash Card Front

TDS Section Number: 194C

Flash Card Back

- Description: Payment to contractors and sub-contractors.

- Rate of TDS: 1% for individuals/HUF, 2% for others.

- Threshold: ₹30,000 for a single transaction, ₹100,000 for aggregate transactions in a year.

You can create similar flash cards for other TDS section numbers like 194J, 194H, etc.

By incorporating these techniques into your study routine, you can enhance your ability to remember section numbers and their details. Practice regularly and find the methods that work best for you. Happy studying! ??

CHAPTER FORTY-ONE

ACTIVE RECALL FOR CA STUDENTS

Active recall is a powerful study technique that involves actively stimulating your memory during the learning process. Instead of passively reviewing notes or textbooks, active recall requires you to retrieve information from memory, which strengthens your ability to remember and understand the material. Here are some strategies for CA students to use active recall effectively:

1. Practice Questions

- Regularly practice past exam questions and mock tests. This helps you simulate exam conditions and reinforces your understanding.

2. Flashcards

- Create flashcards for key concepts and terms. Quiz yourself regularly, trying to recall the information without looking at the answers.

3. Teach Others

- Explain concepts to friends, family, or study groups. Teaching forces you to recall and articulate the material, deepening your understanding.

4. Self-Quizzing

- After studying a topic, close your notes and try to write down everything you remember. This helps identify gaps in your knowledge.

5. Summarization

- Summarize chapters or topics in your own words without referring to the textbook. This helps reinforce key points and concepts.

6. Active Engagement in Study Groups

- Participate in study group discussions where you actively recall and discuss topics with peers. This collaborative effort can provide new insights and reinforce learning.

7. Spaced Repetition

- Use a spaced repetition system (SRS) to review information at increasing intervals. This helps transfer knowledge from short-term to long-term memory.

8. Mind Maps

- Create mind maps to visually organize and recall information. This helps in linking concepts and improving memory retention.

9. Practice Exams

- Take full-length practice exams under timed conditions. This not only helps with recall but also improves time management and exam technique.

Benefits of Active Recall

- Improves Memory: Strengthens neural pathways, making it easier to recall information during exams.

- Enhances Understanding: Helps you grasp and internalize concepts rather than just memorizing facts.

- Boosts Confidence: Regular practice and successful recall build confidence and reduce exam anxiety.

By incorporating active recall into your study routine, you can enhance your learning efficiency and perform better in your CA exams. ??

CHAPTER FORTY-TWO

SPACED REPETITION

Spaced repetition is a highly effective study technique that involves reviewing information at increasing intervals. This method helps transfer knowledge from short-term to long-term memory and is particularly beneficial for CA students who need to retain vast amounts of information over an extended period. Here's how you can implement spaced repetition in your study routine:

1.Break Down Your Study Material

- Divide your syllabus into smaller chunks or topics. This makes it easier to manage and schedule reviews.

2. Create a Study Schedule

- Plan your study sessions in advance, ensuring you revisit each topic multiple times with increasing gaps between sessions. For example:

- Day 1: Initial study session
- Day 2: First review
- Day 4: Second review
- Day 7: Third review
- Day 14: Fourth review

3. Use Flashcards

- Flashcards are an excellent tool for spaced repetition. Write questions on one side and answers on the other. Quiz yourself regularly, increasing the interval between reviews for cards you know well.

4. Utilize Spaced Repetition Software (SRS)

- Tools like Anki or Quizlet can automate the process, scheduling your reviews based on how well you know each piece of information.

5. Active Recall

- Combine spaced repetition with active recall techniques. Instead of simply rereading notes, actively try to recall the information without looking at your notes.

6. Consistent Reviews

- Make reviewing a part of your daily routine. Even a few minutes each day can make a significant difference in retention.

Benefits of Spaced Repetition

- Enhanced Memory Retention: Reinforces learning over time, making it easier to remember information during exams.

- Efficient Learning: Focuses your efforts on the material you struggle with most, saving time and improving overall understanding.

- Reduced Cramming: Regular reviews reduce the need for last-minute cramming and the associated stress.

Example Schedule

Here's an example of how you might structure your spaced repetition for a particular topic:

Day	Activity
Day 1	Initial Study
Day 3	First Review
Day 7	Second Review
Day 14	Third Review
Day 21	Fourth Review

Tips for Success

1. Be Consistent: Stick to your schedule to maximize the benefits.

2. Adjust Intervals: If you find certain topics particularly challenging, shorten the intervals for those.

3. Stay Organized: Keep track of what you've studied and when your next review is due.

By incorporating spaced repetition into your study routine, you can improve your retention and performance in your CA exams. Keep going, and remember that progress is your key to success! ??

CHAPTER FORTY-THREE

TEACHING TO LEARN - THE FEYNMAN TECHNIQUE

The Feynman Technique is a brilliant method developed by the physicist Richard Feynman to help understand complex concepts deeply and clearly. It's particularly useful for CA students who need to master intricate accounting and financial topics. Here's a breakdown of how the Feynman Technique can be applied to your studies:

1. Choose a Concept: Pick a topic you're struggling with or need to understand better. It could be a concept like "Deferred Tax Liability" or "Consolidation of Financial Statements".

2. Teach it to a Child: Explain the concept in simple terms, as if you were teaching it to a child. Avoid jargon and complex terms. This forces you to simplify your understanding.

3. Identify Gaps: While explaining, you'll notice where your understanding is lacking. Go back to your study materials and fill in those gaps.

4. Review and Simplify: Refine your explanation, making it as simple and clear as possible. Use analogies and examples to make the concept more relatable.

5. Teach Someone Else: Find a study partner or a friend and explain the concept to them. Teaching others is one of the most effective ways to reinforce your own understanding.

Applying the Feynman Technique to your CA studies can transform how you learn and retain information, making your preparation more efficient and effective.

CHAPTER FORTY-FOUR

THE MIND MAP TECHNIQUE

The mind map technique is a powerful tool that can help CA students organize their thoughts, simplify complex information, and enhance their memory. Here's how you can effectively use mind mapping for your studies:

Steps to Create a Mind Map

1. Start with a Central Idea

- Write the main topic or concept in the center of the page. For example, if you're studying Financial Accounting, write "Financial Accounting" in the center.

2. Branch Out Major Themes

- Draw branches from the central idea to represent the major themes or topics. For Financial Accounting, these might include "Balance Sheet," "Income Statement," "Cash Flow Statement," and "Accounting Principles."

3. Add Sub-Topics

- From each major theme, draw smaller branches to include sub-topics. For example, under "Balance Sheet," you could have "Assets," "Liabilities," and "Equity."

4. Include Details

- Add further details and examples to each sub-topic. Under "Assets," you could include "Current Assets," "Fixed Assets," and specific examples like "Inventory," "Accounts Receivable," and "Machinery."

5. Use Keywords and Images

- Use keywords, symbols, and images to make the mind map visually appealing and easier to remember. For example, use a dollar sign ($) to represent financial elements or a small drawing of a building for "Fixed Assets."

6. Color Code

- Use different colors for different branches to visually distinguish between various sections. This can help in better retention and recall.

7. Review and Update

- Regularly review and update your mind map as you learn more. Add new information or rearrange branches to reflect a better understanding.

Example Mind Map for CA Students

Here's how you might create a mind map for Financial Accounting:

Central Idea

- Financial Accounting

Major Themes

1. Balance Sheet

- Assets

- Current Assets: Inventory, Accounts Receivable

- Fixed Assets: Machinery, Buildings

- Liabilities

- Short-term Liabilities: Accounts Payable, Short-term Loans

- Long-term Liabilities: Long-term Loans, Bonds

- Equity

- Shareholder's Equity: Common Stock, Retained Earnings

2. Income Statement

- Revenues

- Sales Revenue, Service Revenue

- Expenses

- Cost of Goods Sold, Operating Expenses, Depreciation

3. Cash Flow Statement

- Operating Activities

- Investing Activities

- Financing Activities

4. Accounting Principles

- GAAP

- IFRS

Benefits of Mind Mapping for CA Students

- Organized Information: Mind maps help organize complex information in a structured way, making it easier to study and understand.

- Visual Learning: The visual layout of mind maps caters to visual learners and enhances memory retention.

- Easy Review: Mind maps provide a quick and comprehensive review of entire topics, aiding in effective revision.

- Engagement: The process of creating mind maps is engaging and can make studying more enjoyable.

By incorporating the mind map technique into your study routine, you can enhance your understanding of complex concepts, improve memory retention, and make your study sessions more effective.

CHAPTER FORTY-FIVE

SUBJECT-WISE STRATEGIES TO HELP YOU EXCEL IN THE CA EXAMS:

1. Accounting

- Conceptual Clarity: Focus on understanding fundamental accounting principles and concepts thoroughly.

- Regular Practice: Solve practical problems daily to improve accuracy and speed.

- Summary Notes: Prepare concise notes for each topic for quick revision before exams.

2. Law

- Study Bare Acts: Read and understand the language of the law from the Bare Acts.

- Case Laws: Refer to important case laws and understand their implications.

- Amendments: Stay updated with recent amendments and changes in law.

3. Cost and Management Accounting

- Formulae and Concepts: Memorize important formulae and understand the underlying concepts.

- Application: Practice applying these concepts to different scenarios and case studies.

- Time Management: Practice solving problems within a stipulated time to enhance speed.

4. Taxation

- Income Tax Act: Gain a deep understanding of the Income Tax Act and its provisions.

- Practical Problems: Solve a variety of problems to get accustomed to different tax scenarios.

- GST: Stay updated on Goods and Services Tax (GST) provisions and practice GST-related problems.

5. Advanced Accounting

- Complex Problems: Focus on solving complex accounting problems, including consolidation and amalgamation.

- AS and Ind AS: Understand and remember Accounting Standards (AS) and Indian Accounting Standards (Ind AS).

- Revision: Regularly revise key concepts and standards.

6. Auditing and Assurance

- Audit Procedures: Familiarize yourself with different audit procedures and their applications.

- Standards on Auditing (SAs): Memorize important Standards on Auditing and their key points.

- Report Writing: Practice writing audit reports and understanding the format.

7. Financial Management and Economics for Finance

- Ratio Analysis: Master ratio analysis and its application in financial management.

- Capital Budgeting: Understand the concepts and techniques of capital budgeting thoroughly.

- Economics: Stay updated with current economic scenarios and their impact on finance.

8. Information Technology and Strategic Management

- IT Concepts: Understand key IT concepts, including information systems, databases, and cybersecurity.

- Strategic Management: Study strategic management theories and their practical applications.

- Case Studies: Practice with case studies to apply theoretical concepts.

9. Corporate and Allied Laws

- Companies Act: Gain a thorough understanding of the Companies Act and its provisions.

- Case Laws and Amendments: Stay updated with recent amendments and important case laws.

- Theory and Practical: Balance studying theoretical concepts and practicing practical problems.

10. Direct Tax Laws and International Taxation

- Detailed Study: Focus on understanding detailed provisions of direct tax laws.

- International Taxation: Study international taxation concepts and their applications.

- Updates: Stay updated with recent changes and amendments in tax laws.

11. Indirect Tax Laws

- GST: Gain a deep understanding of GST and its provisions.

- Customs Laws: Study customs laws and their applications.

- Practice: Solve a variety of practical problems to understand different scenarios.

General Tips for All Subjects

- Regular Revision: Schedule regular revision sessions to reinforce your learning.

- Mock Tests: Take mock tests to assess your preparation and improve your time management.

- Time Management: Allocate study time wisely and stick to a study schedule.

- Healthy Routine: Maintain a healthy routine with adequate sleep, exercise, and relaxation.

By following these subject-wise strategies and tips, you can enhance your preparation and increase your chances of success in the CA exams. If you have any more questions or need further assistance, feel free to ask!

CHAPTER FORTY-SIX

SECRETS TO GETTING MORE MARKS IN CA EXAMS

Scoring high marks in the CA exams requires a combination of effective study strategies, discipline, and exam techniques. Here are some key secrets to help you excel:

Secrets to Getting More Marks in CA Exams

1. Thorough Understanding of Syllabus:

- Know Your Syllabus: Be well-versed with the CA syllabus and exam pattern. Understand the weightage of each topic and prioritize accordingly.

- Study Material: Use ICAI study material, RTPs (Revision Test Papers), MTPs (Mock Test Papers), and suggested answers to guide your preparation.

2. Effective Time Management:

- Create a Study Schedule: Plan your study sessions well in advance and stick to a routine. Allocate time based on the complexity and importance of each subject.

- Time Blocking: Use time management techniques to maintain focus and productivity.

3. Active Learning Techniques:

- Active Recall: Test yourself regularly on the topics you've studied. This reinforces memory and helps identify weak areas.

- Spaced Repetition: Review material at regular intervals to retain information over the long term. Tools like Anki can help manage this process.

4. Practice and Revision:

- Solve Past Papers: Practice with past exam papers to get a feel for the types of questions and the exam format. This helps in improving speed and accuracy.

- Mock Tests: Take mock tests under exam conditions to build confidence and reduce exam anxiety.

5. Clear Concepts and Application:

- Understand Concepts: Focus on understanding the core concepts rather than rote learning. This helps in tackling tricky questions effectively.

- Application: Practice applying concepts to practical problems, as CA exams often test practical application skills.

6. Regular Revision:

- Revision Plan: Have a structured revision plan. Review your notes regularly and focus on revising high-weightage topics multiple times.

- Summarize Notes: Create concise notes or mind maps for quick revision before exams.

7. Exam Writing Skills:

- Answer Presentation: Present your answers clearly and concisely. Use headings, subheadings, bullet points, and diagrams where appropriate.

- Time Management in Exams: Allocate time to each question and stick to it. Don't spend too long on any single question.

8. Healthy Lifestyle:

- Balanced Diet and Exercise: Maintain a healthy lifestyle with a balanced diet and regular exercise to keep your mind and body fit.

- Adequate Sleep: Ensure you get enough sleep to stay focused and retain information better.

9. Stay Positive and Motivated:

- Set Goals: Set realistic and achievable study goals. Celebrate small victories to stay motivated.

- Support System: Surround yourself with supportive friends and family who encourage and motivate you.

By following these strategies and maintaining a disciplined approach, you can maximize your performance and achieve higher marks in your CA exams. Best of luck with your studies! ???

CHAPTER FORTY-SEVEN

IMPORTANCE OF HANDWRITING AND PRESENTATION IN CA

Handwriting and presentation play a significant role in CA exams, impacting not only the clarity but also the impression of your answers. Here's why they are crucial:

Importance of Handwriting in CA Exams

1. Clarity and Legibility:

- Readable Answers: Clear and legible handwriting ensures that the examiner can read and understand your answers easily. Poor handwriting can lead to misinterpretation and missed marks.

- First Impressions: Neat handwriting creates a positive first impression, which can influence the examiner's overall perception of your work.

2. Speed and Efficiency:

- Writing Speed: Practicing good handwriting can help you write faster without sacrificing legibility, which is crucial for completing the exam on time.

- Efficiency: Neat handwriting allows you to efficiently review and make corrections to your answers during the exam.

Importance of Presentation in CA Exams

1. Organized Answers:

- Structure and Flow: Well-presented answers with clear headings, subheadings, bullet points, and paragraphs help in organizing thoughts logically and making it easier for the examiner to follow.

- Highlighting Key Points: Use of underlining or highlighting key points draws attention to important parts of your answer, ensuring they are not missed.

2. Professionalism:

- Professional Appearance: A well-presented answer sheet reflects professionalism and attention to detail, traits valued in a Chartered Accountant.

- Enhanced Understanding: Proper presentation enhances the overall understanding of your answers, reducing the chances of ambiguity and errors.

Tips for Improving Handwriting and Presentation

1. Practice Regularly:

- Dedicate time to practice handwriting and presentation techniques. Write sample answers to simulate exam conditions.

2. Use Clear and Consistent Style:

- Adopt a clear and consistent handwriting style. Ensure uniformity in size and spacing of letters.

3. Structure Your Answers:

- Use headings, subheadings, and bullet points to organize your answers. This breaks down information into manageable parts.

4. Highlight Key Points:

- Underline important points and keywords. Use different pen colors if allowed(Guidelines do not allow using different colour hence please refer to the latest guideline).

5. Leave Margins:

- Leave adequate margins on both sides of the answer sheet for clarity and additional notes or corrections.

6. Manage Space:

- Avoid overcrowding your answer sheet. Use sufficient spacing between words, lines, and paragraphs.

7. Review and Edit:

- Allocate time to review your answers for any handwriting or presentation issues. Make necessary corrections for better readability.

Example of Well-Presented Answer:

Question: Explain the concept of Revenue Recognition.

Answer:

1. Definition:

- Revenue recognition is an accounting principle that dictates the specific conditions under which revenue is recognized. It determines how and when revenue is measured and recorded.

2. Key Principles:

- Realization Principle: Revenue is recognized when it is earned and realizable.

- Matching Principle: Revenue is matched with the expenses incurred to generate it.

3. Criteria for Recognition:

- Performance Obligation: Revenue is recognized when the performance obligation is satisfied.

- Transfer of Control: Control of the goods or services must be transferred to the customer.

4. Example:

- For a software company, revenue is recognized when the software is delivered and installed, and the customer has accepted it.

By focusing on both handwriting and presentation, you can enhance the clarity and professionalism of your answers, ultimately improving your chances of scoring higher marks in your CA exams. Keep practicing and refining your skills!

CHAPTER FORTY-EIGHT

MOCK TEST

Mock tests are a great way to prepare for your CA exams! They help you get familiar with the exam format, manage your time effectively, and identify areas where you need improvement. Here are some resources and tips for taking mock tests:

Resources for Mock Tests

1. ICAI BoS Knowledge Portal: The Institute of Chartered Accountants of India (ICAI) provides mock test papers for both Foundation and Intermediate levels. You can access these on the BoS Knowledge Portal.

2. ICAI BOS App: Download the ICAI BOS App to access mock tests and other study materials.

3. Regional Councils and Branches: Check with your local ICAI Regional Council or Branch for any physical mock test sessions.

Tips for Taking Mock Tests

1. Simulate Exam Conditions: Try to recreate the exam environment as closely as possible. Find a quiet place, set a timer, and avoid any distractions.

2. Review Your Answers: After completing a mock test, review your answers and understand the mistakes you made. This will help you avoid them in the actual exam.

3. Analyze Time Management: Keep track of how much time you spend on each question. This will help you manage your time better during the real exam.

4. Practice Regularly: Take mock tests regularly to build your confidence and improve your speed and accuracy.

5. Focus on Weak Areas: Use the results of your mock tests to identify your weak areas and focus your study efforts on improving them.

By incorporating mock tests into your study routine, you can better prepare for the CA exams and increase your chances of success.

How to Access Mock Tests:

1. Visit the ICAI website: Go to the official ICAI website (icai.org) and navigate to the BoS Knowledge Portal.

2. Download Question Papers: The question papers will be uploaded to the portal by 1:30 PM on the scheduled dates.

3. Attempt Mock Tests: Download and attempt the mock tests within the stipulated time limit.

4. Review Answer Keys: The answer keys will be uploaded within 48 hours of the test commencement. Use them to self-assess your performance and identify areas for improvement.

Mock tests are a great way to practice, assess your preparation, and get familiar with the exam pattern. Make sure to take them seriously and use them as a tool to boost your confidence and improve your performance.

Good luck with your preparation!

CHAPTER FORTY-NINE

REVISION TEST PAPER (RTP)

Revision test papers, also known as RTPs (Revision Test Papers), are a valuable resource for CA students to prepare for their exams. These papers are designed by the Institute of Chartered Accountants of India (ICAI) and provide practice questions similar to those that might appear on the actual exam.

How to Access Revision Test Papers

1. ICAI BoS Knowledge Portal: You can access revision test papers for Foundation, Intermediate, and Final levels on the ICAI BoS Knowledge Portal. Here's the link: [ICAI BoS Knowledge Portal](https://boslive.icai.org/education_content.php?p=Revision%20Test%20Papers).

2. ICAI BOS App: Download the ICAI BOS App to access revision test papers and other study materials.

3. Regional Councils and Branches: Check with your local ICAI Regional Council or Branch for any physical mock test sessions or additional resources.

Benefits of Using Revision Test Papers

- Practice Under Exam Conditions: Helps you get used to the exam format and time constraints.

- Identify Weak Areas: Allows you to pinpoint topics that need more attention.

- Boost Confidence: Familiarity with the types of questions can boost your confidence on exam day.

- Effective Revision: Provides a structured way to revise and consolidate your knowledge.

Tips for Using Revision Test Papers

1. Simulate Exam Conditions: Try to recreate the exam environment as closely as possible.

2. Review Your Answers: After completing a test, review your answers and understand any mistakes.

3. Analyze Time Management: Keep track of how much time you spend on each question.

4. Focus on Weak Areas: Use the results to identify and work on your weak areas.

5. Regular Practice: Take revision tests regularly to build your confidence and improve your speed and accuracy.

By incorporating revision test papers into your study routine, you can better prepare for the CA exams and increase your chances of success. Good luck with your preparation!

CHAPTER FIFTY

HANDLING FEAR

Fear is a natural part of the journey for CA students, especially given the rigorous nature of the exams and the high stakes involved. Here are some strategies to help you handle fear and turn it into a driving force for success:

Taking action is a powerful antidote to fear. When you begin to act, the uncertainty and anxiety that often accompany fear start to diminish. The key is to focus on small, manageable steps that move you forward, building confidence and momentum along the way. Remember, courage isn't the absence of fear, but the willingness to move forward despite it.

Fear often serves as an obstacle rather than a benefit. By acknowledging that fear doesn't add value, we can focus on taking proactive steps and making informed decisions. It's about shifting our perspective and channeling our energy into constructive actions rather than letting fear paralyze us.

Remember, acknowledging fear is natural, but letting it control our actions is a choice we can work to change.

Acknowledge and Understand Your Fear

- Acceptance: Accept that feeling fear is normal. It's a common reaction to challenging and important tasks.

- Identify the Source: Understand what specifically is causing your fear. Is it fear of failure, fear of the unknown, or fear of disappointing others? Identifying the root cause can help you address it more effectively.

Positive Mindset and Self-Talk

- Affirmations: Use positive affirmations to boost your confidence. Remind yourself of your strengths and past successes.

- Reframe Negative Thoughts: Transform negative thoughts into positive ones. Instead of thinking, "I can't do this," tell yourself, "I am capable and well-prepared."

Preparation and Planning

- Effective Study Plan: Create a structured study plan that covers all topics. Break your study sessions into manageable chunks to avoid feeling overwhelmed.

- Practice and Revision: Regular practice and thorough revision can build your confidence and reduce fear. Familiarize yourself with the exam format and types of questions.

Relaxation Techniques

- Deep Breathing: Practice deep breathing exercises to calm your mind and body. This can help reduce anxiety and improve focus.

- Mindfulness and Meditation: Engage in mindfulness or meditation practices to stay present and manage stress.

Support System

- Talk to Someone: Share your fears and concerns with friends, family, or mentors. Talking about your feelings can provide emotional support and perspective.

- Study Groups: Join or form study groups with fellow students. Collaborative learning can ease the burden and provide mutual encouragement.

Visualization and Goal Setting

- Visualize Success: Visualize yourself successfully completing the exams. Imagine the sense of accomplishment and relief you will feel.

- Set Realistic Goals: Set achievable goals for each study session and celebrate small victories. This keeps you motivated and focused.

Healthy Lifestyle

- Balanced Diet: Eat a nutritious diet to keep your body and mind in optimal condition.

- Regular Exercise: Incorporate physical activity into your routine. Exercise helps reduce stress and boosts your mood.

- Adequate Sleep: Ensure you get enough rest. A well-rested mind is better equipped to handle stress and fear.

Seek Professional Help if Needed

- Counseling: If fear and anxiety become overwhelming, consider seeking help from a counselor or health professional. They can provide strategies and support to manage your fears.

Final Thoughts

Fear is not something to be eradicated but managed and used as a motivator. By adopting these strategies, you can transform your fear into a powerful ally on your journey to becoming a Chartered Accountant. Remember, it's okay to feel scared, but with the right approach, you can overcome it and achieve your goals. Stay strong and keep moving forward!

CHAPTER FIFTY-ONE

TAP INTO YOUR UNTAPPED POTENTIAL

According to an ancient Hindu legend, in the beginning, all humans were gods and possessed divine powers. However, they misused these powers, causing chaos in the world. To protect the universe, Brahma, the creator of the universe, decided to hide these divine powers where humans could not easily find them.

Brahma called a meeting of the gods to discuss where to hide the powers. One god suggested hiding the powers deep in the earth, but Brahma thought that humans would eventually dig deep enough to find them. Another suggested hiding them in the depths of the ocean, but Brahma knew that humans would explore the ocean depths.

Finally, Brahma had a brilliant idea. He said, "I will hide the divine powers within humans themselves. They will never think to look there." The gods agreed, and so Brahma hid the divine powers within the human brain. From that day forward, humans have had to embark on a journey of self-discovery to realize their true potential.

Lessons for CA Students

1. Recognize Your Inner Potential

- Divine Power Within: Just as Brahma hid divine power within humans, CA students should recognize that they possess immense potential within themselves.

- Action: Believe in your abilities and trust that you have the capacity to achieve your goals.

2. Embark on a Journey of Self-Discovery

- Journey to Find Power: The story emphasizes the importance of self-discovery. CA students should continuously seek to understand their strengths and weaknesses.

- Action: Engage in self-reflection and personal development activities to uncover and harness your true potential.

3. Persevere Through Challenges

- Hidden Power: The divine power is not easily accessible; it requires effort and perseverance to uncover. Similarly, achieving success in the CA exams requires determination and hard work.

- Action: Stay committed to your studies and persevere through challenges, knowing that your efforts will lead to success.

4. Use Your Abilities Wisely

- Misuse of Powers: The story began with humans misusing their divine powers. CA students should use their knowledge and skills ethically and responsibly.

- Action: Apply your accounting knowledge to make a positive impact and uphold ethical standards in your profession.

5. Continuous Learning and Growth

- Eternal Quest: The journey of self-discovery is ongoing. CA students should embrace lifelong learning and continuously strive for improvement.

- Action: Stay curious, keep learning, and seek opportunities for growth both professionally and personally.

By embracing the lessons from the story of Brahma hiding the divine power, CA students can unlock their inner potential, persevere through challenges, and achieve their academic and professional goals.

CHAPTER FIFTY-TWO

WHICH ANIMAL YOU ARE FEEDING? -THE STORY OF THE TWO WOLVES

The concept of two minds fighting within us is often illustrated by the story of the Two Wolves, which can be quite insightful for CA students as well. Here's how the story goes and the lessons it imparts:

The Story of the Two Wolves

An old Cherokee chief was teaching his grandson about life. "A fight is going on inside me," he said to the boy. "It is a terrible fight, and it is between two wolves. One is evil—he is anger, envy, sorrow, regret, greed, arrogance, self-pity, guilt, resentment, inferiority, lies, false pride, superiority, and ego."

He continued, "The other is good—he is joy, peace, love, hope, serenity, humility, kindness, benevolence, empathy, generosity, truth, compassion, and faith. The same fight is going on inside you—and inside every other person, too."

The grandson thought about it for a minute and then asked his grandfather, "Which wolf will win?"

The old chief simply replied, "The one you feed."

Lessons for CA Students

1. Mindset Matters

- Two Wolves Within: The story highlights the internal battle between positive and negative thoughts. CA students should be mindful of their thoughts and focus on nurturing positivity.

- Action: Practice positive self-talk and affirmations. Remind yourself of your strengths and accomplishments.

2. Focus on the Positive

- Feeding the Right Wolf: Just as the Cherokee chief explained, focusing on positive qualities and emotions can help you thrive.

- Action: Engage in activities that bring you joy and fulfillment. Surround yourself with supportive people who uplift you.

3. Overcome Negative Emotions

- Acknowledging Negative Emotions: It's important to acknowledge negative emotions but not let them control you. Learn to manage them effectively.

- Action: Develop healthy coping mechanisms such as mindfulness, meditation, or talking to a mentor or friend when you feel overwhelmed.

4. Cultivate Resilience

- Strengthening the Good Wolf: Building resilience is about strengthening your positive attributes and staying hopeful even in challenging times.

- Action: Reflect on past challenges you've overcome and recognize your ability to handle adversity.

Practical Steps for CA Students

1. Mindfulness Practices: Incorporate mindfulness or meditation into your daily routine to maintain mental clarity and focus.

2. Gratitude Journaling: Keep a gratitude journal to remind yourself of the positive aspects of your life and studies.

3. Positive Visualization: Visualize your success and the steps needed to achieve your goals. This can boost confidence and motivation.

4. Healthy Lifestyle: Maintain a balanced diet, exercise regularly, and get enough sleep to support both physical and mental well-being.

By feeding the positive "wolf" within, CA students can foster a constructive mindset, enhance resilience, and navigate their studies with greater confidence and optimism. ??

Which "wolf" are you feeding today?

CHAPTER FIFTY-THREE

POSITIVE AFFIRMATIONS

Positive affirmations can significantly benefit CA students by fostering a mindset of growth and resilience. Repeating encouraging statements helps to build self-confidence, reduce stress, and maintain motivation during the rigorous preparation for exams. They act as mental boosts that can transform negative thoughts into positive ones, promoting a sense of empowerment and focus. By regularly practicing positive affirmations, CA students can enhance their overall well-being and academic performance, making the challenging journey more manageable and fulfilling.

Here are some positive affirmations to keep you motivated and focused:

1. "I am capable and well-prepared to pass my CA exams."
2. "Every challenge I face is an opportunity to grow and learn."
3. "I believe in my abilities and my dedication."
4. "I am focused, determined, and persistent."
5. "My hard work and effort will pay off."
6. "I learn and retain information easily."
7. "I am calm, confident, and in control."
8. "I will overcome any obstacle in my path."
9. "I trust the process and my progress."
10. "I am one step closer to achieving my goal every day."
11. "I am resilient and can handle any pressure."
12. "I am proud of my commitment and dedication."
13. "I am constantly improving and growing."
14. "Success is a journey, and I am on the right path."
15. "I have the knowledge and skills to succeed."

Repeat these affirmations daily to stay positive and motivated throughout your CA journey. You've got this!

CHAPTER FIFTY-FOUR

POSITIVE VISUALIZATIONS FOR SUCCESS

Positive visualizations can be a powerful tool for CA students to boost confidence, reduce stress, and enhance performance during exams. Here are some visualization techniques that can help:

1. Visualization of Success

Picture yourself in the examination hall, feeling calm and confident. Imagine yourself answering each question with ease and clarity. Visualize the moment when you receive your results and see that you have passed with flying colors. Feel the pride and satisfaction of your hard work paying off.

2. Daily Affirmations

Create a set of positive affirmations related to your studies and exam success. For example, "I am prepared and confident," "I understand and retain all the concepts I study," and "I will excel in my CA exams." Repeat these affirmations daily while visualizing yourself achieving your goals.

3. Visualization of Study Sessions

Visualize your study sessions as productive and efficient. See yourself understanding complex concepts easily and retaining the information. Imagine yourself being focused and motivated during your study time.

4. Stress Management Visualization

When you feel stressed, visualize a calming and peaceful place, such as a beach or a forest. Imagine yourself there, feeling relaxed and free from anxiety. Practice deep breathing while you visualize this place to help manage exam-related stress.

5. Goal Visualization

Set specific, achievable goals for your CA exams. Visualize yourself reaching these goals step by step. For example, if your goal is to complete a particular chapter by the end of the week, visualize yourself studying that chapter and understanding it thoroughly.

6. Visualization of Exam Day Routine

Visualize your exam day from start to finish. See yourself waking up early, having a healthy breakfast, reviewing your notes confidently, and arriving at the exam center feeling prepared. Imagine yourself going through the exam smoothly and finishing it with a sense of accomplishment.

7. Visualization of Overcoming Challenges

Visualize yourself overcoming any challenges that might come your way. Whether it's a tough question or a moment of self-doubt, see yourself handling it with confidence and resilience. Imagine yourself finding solutions and pushing through any obstacles.

Visualization Practice

Take a few minutes each day to practice these visualizations. Find a quiet place, close your eyes, and immerse yourself in the positive images and feelings. Consistent practice can reinforce your confidence and improve your performance.

By incorporating these positive visualizations into your routine, you'll be better equipped to approach your CA exams with a positive mindset and a greater sense of confidence. You've got this! ?

CHAPTER FIFTY-FIVE

GRATITUDE TO STAY MOTIVATED

Practicing gratitude can be a powerful way to stay motivated and maintain a positive mindset during your CA journey. Here are some gratitude practices and affirmations specifically for CA students:

Gratitude Practices

1. Daily Gratitude Journal:

- Write down three things you're grateful for every day, whether related to your studies or personal life.

2. Gratitude Visualization:

- Spend a few minutes each day visualizing the people, opportunities, and resources that support your journey.

3. Gratitude Meditation:

- During your meditation, focus on the feeling of gratitude. Picture yourself surrounded by positive energy and thankfulness.

4. Thank-You Notes:

- Write thank-you notes to mentors, teachers, or peers who have helped you. This not only spreads positivity but also reinforces your gratitude.

Gratitude Affirmations

1. I am grateful for the knowledge and skills I am gaining each day.

2. I appreciate the support and encouragement from my family, friends, and mentors.

3. I am thankful for the challenges that help me grow and improve.

4. I am grateful for the opportunities to learn and advance in my career.

5. I appreciate the journey and the progress I am making, no matter how small.

6. I am thankful for my resilience and dedication to my goals.

7. I am grateful for the clarity and focus I bring to my studies.

8. I appreciate the resources and tools that help me succeed.

9. I am thankful for the strength and determination I show every day.

10. I am grateful for the ability to pursue my dreams and achieve my goals.

Incorporating these gratitude practices and affirmations into your daily routine can help you stay positive and focused on your CA journey. Remember to celebrate your progress and be kind to yourself along the way. You are doing great!

CHAPTER FIFTY-SIX

THE 5-SECOND RULE FOR RAPID RESPONSE

The 5-second rule is a simple yet powerful technique to overcome procrastination and take immediate action. Here's how CA students can use it effectively:

How to Use the 5-Second Rule

1. Identify the Task: Recognize the task or activity you need to start, whether it's studying, practicing past papers, or attending a class.

2. Countdown: When you feel the urge to procrastinate, count backward from 5 to 1 in your mind: 5, 4, 3, 2, 1.

3. Take Action: Once you reach 1, launch yourself into action without hesitation.

Benefits for CA Students

- Break Procrastination: The 5-second countdown interrupts your habit of overthinking and pushes you to start tasks immediately.

- Increase Productivity: By taking immediate action, you'll get more done in less time, helping you manage your study schedule better.

- Boost Confidence: Each time you successfully use the rule, you reinforce your ability to control your actions and build confidence in your self-discipline.

- Enhance Focus: This technique helps you shift your focus from doubts and distractions to taking concrete steps towards your goals.

Example Scenarios

1. Starting a Study Session:

- You know you need to study but feel tempted to browse social media instead. Start the countdown: 5, 4, 3, 2, 1 and open your study material.

2. Practice Mock Tests:

- If you're putting off taking a mock test, use the countdown to motivate yourself to begin: 5, 4, 3, 2, 1 and start the test.

3. Reviewing Difficult Topics:

- When you're avoiding a challenging subject, countdown: 5, 4, 3, 2, 1 and dive into reviewing those topics.

By consistently using the 5-second rule, you can develop a habit of taking prompt action, ultimately leading to better preparation and performance in your CA exams. Give it a try and see how it transforms your study habits!

CHAPTER FIFTY-SEVEN

MASTER THE ART OF SINGLE-TASKING: FOCUS, PRECISION, SUCCESS

Imagine trying to juggle multiple balls in the air. At first, it might seem thrilling to keep so many objects in motion, but soon, the challenge becomes evident. Each ball demands attention, coordination, and precision. As the number of balls increases, so does the likelihood of dropping one—or all of them. This juggling act serves as a metaphor for multitasking.

Our minds are like the juggler, designed to focus on one ball—one task—at a time. When we try to juggle too many tasks simultaneously, our cognitive resources become strained. We may drop the ball, making mistakes or producing lower quality work. Conversely, when we concentrate on a single ball, we can control it with finesse, ensuring that each catch and throw is precise. This focused approach allows us to excel in one task, leading to better outcomes and more effective performance.

The human brain is often more efficient when it focuses on one task at a time. This concept, known as "single-tasking," can significantly enhance productivity and reduce stress. Here's why focusing on one task at a time can be beneficial:

Focusing on one thing at a time is crucial for CA students due to the complexity and volume of the material.

Benefits of Focusing on One Thing at a Time

1. Increased Concentration: When you focus on a single task, you can give it your undivided attention, leading to a deeper understanding.

2. Reduced Stress: Juggling multiple tasks can be overwhelming. By tackling one thing at a time, you can reduce stress and anxiety.

3. Better Quality Work: Concentrating on one task ensures you perform it to the best of your ability, leading to better results.

How to Practice Single-Tasking

1. Prioritize Your Tasks:

- List out all the tasks you need to complete.

- Prioritize them based on deadlines and importance.

2. Create a Study Schedule:

- Allocate specific time blocks for each subject or topic.

- Stick to the schedule to ensure you cover everything without rushing.

3. Eliminate Distractions:

- Find a quiet study space.

- Turn off notifications on your devices to maintain focus.

4. Use the Time Blocking Technique:

- Study for 25 minutes, then take a 5-minute break.

- This can help maintain focus and prevent burnout.

5. Set Clear Goals:

- Define what you want to achieve in each study session.

- Break down larger tasks into smaller, manageable steps.

6. Take Regular Breaks:

- Short breaks between study sessions help you stay fresh and focused.

- Use breaks to relax and recharge.

Practical Steps

- Morning: Focus on a complex topic when your mind is fresh.

- Afternoon: Review and practice problems related to the morning's topic.

- Evening: Engage in light reading or summary notes to reinforce learning.

By following these steps and focusing on one thing at a time, you'll enhance your productivity and retain information more effectively. Keep at it, and you'll see significant improvements in your studies and overall performance. ?

CHAPTER FIFTY-EIGHT

THE HEROIC GESTURE: BURN THE SHIPS, NO RETRET

In 1519, Spanish conquistador Hernán Cortés landed on the shores of Mexico with a small force of around 600 men. His mission was daunting: to conquer the vast Aztec Empire. Upon landing, Cortés made a radical decision that would become legendary: he ordered his men to burn their ships.

The Decision:

- No Turning Back: By burning the ships, Cortés eliminated any possibility of retreat. His men had no option but to move forward and face the challenges ahead.

- Commitment: This act symbolized total commitment to their mission. The soldiers had to give their all, knowing that their only chance of survival and success lay in conquering the Aztec Empire.

Outcome:

- Unwavering Focus: With no means of escape, Cortés's men were fully focused on their objective. They fought with unparalleled determination and resilience.

- Ultimate Success: Despite overwhelming odds, Cortés and his men eventually succeeded in their mission, leading to the fall of the Aztec Empire.

Lesson for CA Students

The story of Cortés burning the ships serves as a powerful metaphor for CA students:

1. Total Commitment:

- Like Cortés's men, commit fully to your CA journey. Eliminate any thoughts of giving up or retreating.

2. Unwavering Focus:

- Stay focused on your goals. Dedicate your time and energy to studying, practicing, and mastering the subjects.

3. Resilience and Determination:

- Embrace challenges and setbacks as part of the journey. Use them to strengthen your resolve and determination.

4. No Plan B:

- Treat your CA preparation as if there's no Plan B. Pour all your efforts into ensuring success, knowing that perseverance is your only option.

By adopting this mindset, you can tackle the rigorous demands of the CA course with the same determination and focus that led Cortés and his men to victory.

Remember, the journey may be tough, but with unwavering commitment and resilience, you can achieve your goal of becoming a Chartered Accountant. Keep pushing forward, and believe in your ability to succeed! ??

CHAPTER FIFTY-NINE

PATIENCE AND PERSISTENCE

Patience and persistence are key ingredients for success, especially in demanding exams like the CA. Here's how these qualities can make a difference:

Patience:

1. Learning Takes Time: Understanding complex accounting concepts and principles doesn't happen overnight. Be patient with yourself as you navigate through difficult topics.

2. Practice and Repetition: It's normal to not grasp everything on the first try. Continuous practice and revision are essential.

3. Stay Calm Under Pressure: During exams, maintaining a calm and patient mindset can help you think clearly and avoid mistakes.

Persistence:

1. Consistent Effort: Regular and dedicated study sessions contribute to long-term understanding and retention.

2. Overcoming Challenges: There will be tough topics and setbacks. Persistence helps you push through these obstacles rather than giving up.

3. Long-Term Goals: The journey to becoming a CA is long and challenging. Persistence keeps you motivated to keep going until you achieve your goal.

Tips for Cultivating Patience and Persistence:

- Set Realistic Goals: Break down your study material into manageable chunks and set achievable goals.

- Celebrate Small Wins: Acknowledge and reward yourself for the small milestones you reach along the way.

- Stay Organized: Keep a study schedule and stick to it. This helps in maintaining a steady and persistent study routine.

- Seek Support: Don't hesitate to ask for help from peers, mentors, or tutors when you're stuck. Sharing knowledge can make the process easier.

- Mindfulness and Stress Management: Practice techniques like deep breathing, meditation, or yoga to manage stress and maintain patience.

Remember, every step you take, no matter how small, brings you closer to your goal. Keep moving forward, one day at a time.?

CHAPTER SIXTY

THE STORY OF A DIAMOND

The journey of a diamond, from a piece of carbon to a sparkling gem, is a beautiful metaphor for CA students' journey. Here's how the story goes.

A diamond starts as carbon buried deep within the earth. Through immense pressure and extreme temperatures over millions of years, the carbon transforms into a rough diamond. This rough diamond is then mined, cut, and polished to reveal its brilliance.

Lessons for CA Students

1. Transformation Through Pressure

- Just like carbon transforms into a diamond under pressure, CA students must endure the pressures of rigorous study and exams to emerge stronger and more capable.

2. Patience and Time

- The formation of a diamond takes millions of years, symbolizing the importance of patience. Your journey to becoming a CA will take time and consistent effort.

3. Cutting and Polishing

- Once mined, a rough diamond undergoes cutting and polishing to bring out its brilliance. Similarly, continuous learning, practice, and refinement of your skills will reveal your true potential.

4. Inner Strength

- Despite its outward appearance, a diamond's true value lies in its inner structure. For CA students, inner strength, resilience, and determination are key to success.

Applying the Lessons to Your CA Journey

1. Embrace Challenges: Understand that the pressures and challenges you face are shaping you into a stronger and more capable professional.

2. Be Patient: Success takes time. Be patient with yourself and trust the process.

3. Continuous Improvement: Like a diamond being cut and polished, continuously work on improving your knowledge and skills.

4. Inner Resilience: Draw on your inner strength and resilience to overcome obstacles and stay motivated.

By seeing yourself as a diamond in the making, you can stay focused, resilient, and motivated throughout your CA journey. Remember, the pressures you face are transforming you into something brilliant and valuable. ??

Ready to shine through your journey with the brilliance of a diamond?

CHAPTER SIXTY-ONE

THE STORY OF THE BAMBOO TREE

There is a story about the Chinese Bamboo Tree that beautifully illustrates the power of patience and persistence.

In the beginning, a farmer plants the seed of a Chinese Bamboo Tree and nurtures it with water, soil, and sunlight. Despite the farmer's diligent care, nothing happens for the first year. There are no signs of growth, and the ground looks as barren as ever. Undeterred, the farmer continues to care for the seed.

The second year passes, and still no growth. The third and fourth years come and go with no visible progress. By this time, people might begin to wonder why the farmer persists. But the farmer knows that patience and perseverance are key.

Finally, in the fifth year, the tree begins to show signs of growth. Within six weeks, it shoots up to an astonishing height of 80 feet! The rapid growth was only possible because of the strong foundation that had been developing underground for all those years.

Lessons for CA Students

1. Patience and Persistence: Just like the farmer, CA students need to be patient and persistent. Success may not come immediately, but continuous effort will eventually yield results.

2. Strong Foundation: Building a strong foundation of knowledge is crucial. Even if progress seems slow, remember that you are laying the groundwork for future success.

3. Resilience in Adversity: The farmer's unwavering faith and resilience are key to overcoming adversity. Believe in your efforts and stay committed to your goals.

By adopting these strategies and drawing inspiration from the story of the Chinese Bamboo Tree, CA students can handle adversity with resilience and determination. Remember, your hard work and persistence will eventually lead to success. ??

CHAPTER SIXTY-TWO

THE STORY OF A STONE TURNING INTO AN IDOL

The story of a stone turning into an idol can be a powerful metaphor for CA students, representing the transformation through hard work, patience, and persistence.

The Journey of the Stone

Once upon a time, there was a humble stone lying unnoticed by the side of a temple. People walked by it every day, never giving it a second glance. The stone longed to be something more than just a piece of rock.

One day, a skilled sculptor visited the temple. He had an eye for potential and saw something special in the stone. With great care, he picked it up and took it to his workshop. The stone was excited but also apprehensive about what lay ahead.

The sculptor began his work. He chiseled away at the stone, piece by piece. The stone felt the pain of every strike, and at times, it wanted to cry out and ask the sculptor to stop. But the sculptor was relentless; he knew that the only way to reveal the stone's true potential was through this process.

Days turned into weeks, and weeks into months. The stone endured the constant hammering and chiseling, learning to be patient and trusting the sculptor's vision. Slowly, it began to see the transformation taking place. The rough edges smoothed out, and a beautiful form started to emerge.

Finally, after many months of persistent effort, the sculptor stepped back to admire his work. The stone had transformed into a magnificent idol. It was placed in the temple, where people from far and wide came to admire and seek blessings.

The stone, now an idol, realized that the pain and effort were worth it. It had to undergo a challenging process to reveal its true beauty and purpose.

Moral for CA Students

- Patience and Persistence: Just like the stone, your journey to becoming a CA requires patience and persistence. The process might be tough, and there will be moments of doubt and difficulty, but enduring these challenges is what shapes your success.

- Trust the Process: Have faith in the process and trust your abilities. Each concept you master and each exam you take is a step towards revealing your true potential.

- Transformation: The hardships you face are like the sculptor's chisel, shaping you into a more knowledgeable and skilled professional. Embrace the challenges as opportunities to grow and transform.

Remember, every successful CA was once a student who persisted through the chiseling process. Keep pushing forward, and you'll find yourself standing tall as a successful Chartered Accountant, admired for your knowledge and dedication.

CHAPTER SIXTY-THREE

THE 80/20 RULE, THE PARETO PRINCIPLE

The 80/20 rule, also known as the Pareto Principle, suggests that roughly 80% of the results come from 20% of the efforts. CA students can apply this principle to maximize their efficiency and effectiveness. Here's how:

Applying the 80/20 Rule

1. Identify High-Impact Areas:

- Focus on key topics that are most likely to appear in exams. These topics usually cover a significant portion of the syllabus.

- Prioritize subjects or chapters that you find most challenging or are historically high-scoring.

2. Efficient Study Techniques:

- Use active learning methods like summarizing, questioning, and teaching others. This can yield better results than passive reading.

- Implement spaced repetition for memory retention. Review crucial concepts regularly rather than cramming.

3. Practice with Purpose:

- Spend more time on practicing high-yield problems and mock tests that closely mirror exam conditions.

- Analyze past exam papers to understand patterns and prioritize frequently tested areas.

4. Time Management:

- Allocate more study time to the 20% of topics that will likely yield 80% of the results.

- Create a study schedule that includes focused study sessions on these high-impact areas.

5. Minimize Distractions:

- Eliminate or reduce activities that do not contribute significantly to your exam preparation.

- Use tools and techniques to stay focused, like the Pomodoro Technique or designated study hours.

Practical Steps

- Morning Session: Focus on key concepts and difficult topics.

- Afternoon Session: Practice high-yield questions and past papers.

- Evening Session: Review summaries and revisit challenging areas.

By applying the 80/20 rule, you can streamline your efforts and focus on what truly matters, leading to more efficient and effective exam preparation. Keep your eye on the most impactful 20%, and you'll see a significant improvement in your results. Keep pushing forward, you're doing great!

CHAPTER SIXTY-FOUR

THE 2-MINUTE LAUNCHPAD: INITIATE WITH EASE AND BUILD MOMENTUM

The 2-Minute Launchpad Rule and starting rituals are fantastic techniques to get over the initial inertia of studying, especially when juggling multiple subjects. Here's how you can apply these methods to your CA studies:

The 2-Minute Rule:

- What is it?: If a task takes less than 2 minutes, do it now. For tasks that require more time, the rule suggests just starting with 2 minutes.

- Application:

- Start Small: Begin your study session by dedicating just 2 minutes to a subject. Often, the hardest part is starting, and once you do, you'll likely continue beyond those 2 minutes.

- Micro Tasks: Break down larger study tasks into smaller chunks that can be accomplished in 2 minutes. This could be reviewing a single flashcard, summarizing a paragraph, or solving a quick problem.

Starting Rituals:

- What is it?: A specific routine or set of actions you perform to signal the start of a study session. It helps build consistency and a positive habit.

- Application:

- Consistency: Choose a consistent time and place to study. This creates a habit and your brain will be conditioned to focus during this time.

- Preparation: Organize your study materials and workspace beforehand. A clutter-free and prepared space can make starting easier.

- Mindfulness: Spend a few minutes in mindfulness or meditation to clear your mind and prepare for studying. This can be particularly useful before tackling difficult subjects.

- Physical Cues: Actions like making a cup of tea, lighting a candle, or even a short exercise can act as physical cues to signal your brain that it's time to study.

Combining these methods, you could start each study session with a quick 2-minute task to get you going, followed by a brief ritual to maintain consistency and focus. Over time, these habits can significantly improve your productivity and make handling multiple subjects feel more manageable.

CHAPTER SIXTY-FIVE

MENTOR- ILLUMINATING THE PATH TO EXCELLENCE

Having a mentor can be immensely beneficial for CA (Chartered Accountancy) students. A mentor provides invaluable guidance and support throughout the rigorous CA journey, helping students navigate the complexities of the course. They offer expert insights, share practical experiences, and provide tips on how to approach exams and manage time effectively. Mentors can also serve as role models, inspiring students with their achievements and motivating them to stay focused on their goals. Furthermore, they can assist with career planning and networking opportunities, connecting students with industry professionals and potential job prospects. Overall, having a mentor can significantly enhance a CA student's learning experience, boosting their confidence and increasing their chances of success.

Selecting the right mentor is crucial for your success in the CA exam. Here are some key factors to consider when choosing a mentor:

1. Expertise and Experience

- Qualifications: Ensure your mentor is a qualified Chartered Accountant with a deep understanding of the subjects you need help with.

- Experience: Look for someone who has a proven track record of success in the CA exams and has mentored other students successfully.

2. Teaching Style

- Compatibility: Choose a mentor whose teaching style matches your learning preferences. Some students prefer structured lessons, while others thrive in a more flexible, discussion-based approach.iop

- Communication Skills: Your mentor should be able to explain complex concepts in a way that you can easily understand.

3. Availability

- Time Commitment: Ensure your mentor has enough time to dedicate to your learning and can provide timely assistance when you need it.

- Accessibility: Consider how accessible your mentor is for queries, whether through in-person meetings, online sessions, or messages.

4. Mentorship Approach

- Supportive and Encouraging: A good mentor should not only teach but also motivate and inspire you. They should encourage you to stay positive and persistent.

- Constructive Feedback: Look for a mentor who provides honest and constructive feedback, helping you to improve continuously.

5. Personal Connection

- Trust and Rapport: It's important to feel comfortable with your mentor. A strong personal connection can enhance your learning experience.

- Motivational Influence: A mentor who shares their own experiences and challenges can be a great source of inspiration.

6. Recommendations

- References and Testimonials: Seek recommendations from other CA students or professionals who have successfully cleared the exams with the help of a mentor. Testimonials can provide insights into the mentor's effectiveness.

7. Professional Network

- Industry Connections: A mentor with a good professional network can provide valuable career advice and opportunities beyond the exams.

Conclusion

Choosing the right mentor can make a significant difference in your CA exam preparation. Take your time to evaluate potential mentors and select someone who aligns with your needs and goals. Remember, the right mentor will guide you not just academically, but also support you in building confidence and resilience throughout your journey.

NURTURING THE ENVIRONMENT FOR SUCCESS

Environment is key for CA students to maximize focus, productivity, and well-being. Here are some practical tips for environment management:

Environment Management Tips for CA Students

1. Organized Study Space:

- Keep your study area tidy and organized. A clutter-free environment reduces distractions and helps maintain focus. Use shelves, organizers, and drawers to keep your materials in order.

2. Comfortable Furniture:

- Invest in a comfortable chair and desk. Ergonomic furniture can prevent back pain and enhance your comfort during long study sessions.

3. Good Lighting:

- Ensure your study area is well-lit. Natural light is best, but if that's not possible, use a good quality desk lamp to reduce eye strain.

4. Quiet Zone:

- Choose a quiet place for studying where you won't be disturbed. Inform your family or roommates about your study schedule to minimize interruptions.

5. Minimize Distractions:

- Remove potential distractions from your study area. This includes turning off notifications on your devices, using noise-cancelling headphones, and keeping non-study-related items out of sight.

6. Study Materials:

- Have all necessary study materials at hand. This includes textbooks, notes, stationery, and digital devices. Being prepared can save you from unnecessary interruptions.

7. Temperature Control:

- Ensure your study area is at a comfortable temperature. Being too hot or too cold can distract you and affect your concentration.

8. Inspirational Elements:

- Add some motivational quotes, posters, or a vision board in your study space. Positive and inspiring elements can boost your motivation and keep you focused on your goals.

9. Healthy Snacks and Water:

- Keep a bottle of water and some healthy snacks like fruits, nuts, or yogurt nearby. Staying hydrated and having quick access to nutritious snacks can keep your energy levels up.

10. Break Area:

- Designate a separate area for breaks. Stepping away from your study space during breaks can help refresh your mind and prevent burnout.

Example Setup for a Productive Study Environment:

1. Desk and Chair:

- Ergonomic chair with good back support

- Spacious desk with enough room for your laptop, books, and notes

2. Lighting:

- Desk lamp with adjustable brightness

- Position your desk near a window for natural light, if possible

3. Organization:

- Use desk organizers for stationery

- Shelves or cabinets for books and files

- A whiteboard or bulletin board for notes and reminders

4. Decoration:

- Motivational quotes or posters on the wall

- A small plant to add a touch of nature

5. Technology:

- Laptop or computer with necessary software and internet access

- Noise-cancelling headphones for focused study sessions

6. Hydration and Nutrition:

- Water bottle within reach

- Healthy snacks like fruits, nuts, or yogurt on a side table

By creating an environment that supports your study habits, you can enhance your focus, productivity, and overall academic performance. Keep experimenting with what works best for you, and make adjustments as needed. Happy studying!

EMBRACE THE JOURNEY: DISCIPLINE IS ABOUT PROGRESS, NOT PERFECTION.

Discipline guides us on a path where progress shines brighter than perfection. Each step forward is a victory, a testament to growth and persistence. The journey matters more than flawless execution.

Like water wearing down rock overtime, discipline shapes our path with steady progress. Each drop of effort may seem small, but over time, it carves out remarkable change. Perfection is an illusion; it's the consistent, gentle flow that transforms. Celebrate your enduring journey and the progress that gradually shapes your success.

Understanding that progress is more important than perfection is crucial. Here's why:

1. Consistent Effort: Progress comes from consistent, disciplined study habits. Focus on regular study sessions, rather than waiting for perfect conditions or a flawless understanding before moving on.

2. Learning from Mistakes: Embrace mistakes as part of the learning process. Each mistake is an opportunity to learn and improve.

3. Avoid Burnout: Striving for perfection can lead to burnout. Instead, celebrate small victories and improvements, which keep you motivated and energized.

4. Building Confidence: Acknowledge and appreciate your progress. Seeing how far you've come boosts your confidence and keeps you focused

on your goals.

Practical Tips for CA Students:

- Set Realistic Goals: Break down your study material into manageable chunks and set achievable goals.

- Track Your Progress: Keep a journal or use an app to track your daily progress. Reflect on how much you've learned over time.

- Be Kind to Yourself: Understand that perfection is unattainable and self-compassion is key to sustaining long-term success.

- Continuous Improvement: Focus on continuous improvement rather than perfection. Each step forward, no matter how small, is a victory.

Remember, the journey to becoming a Chartered Accountant is a marathon, not a sprint. Consistent progress, fueled by discipline, is what will ultimately lead to your success. Keep moving forward, one step at a time. You've got this! ?

CHAPTER SIXTY-EIGHT

CONSISTENCY: THE QUIET FORCE BEHIND LASTING SUCCESS.

Consistency is the quiet force behind lasting success, often overlooked in favor of more dramatic displays of effort. Unlike intensity, which can be exhausting and unsustainable, consistency embodies the power of steady, unwavering commitment. It's the daily, seemingly small actions that compound over time to yield significant results. Whether it's practicing a skill, maintaining a healthy lifestyle, or building relationships, consistent effort ensures gradual and sustainable progress. This steadfast approach not only builds resilience but also ingrains habits that lead to long-term achievements. By valuing consistency over sporadic bursts of intensity, we create a solid foundation for enduring success and fulfillment.

Consistency over intensity is crucial for CA students, and here's why it makes such a significant difference:

1. Sustainable Learning:

- Long-term Retention: Consistent study habits lead to better retention and understanding of complex subjects. Intense, sporadic study sessions often result in burnout and superficial learning.

- Gradual Progress: Regular, steady study helps in gradually building up knowledge and skills, which is more effective than cramming all at once.

2. Reduced Stress and Anxiety:

- Manageable Workloads: Breaking down the syllabus into smaller, manageable chunks reduces the stress associated with last-minute studying.

- Healthy Routine: Consistent study routines help in maintaining a balanced lifestyle, reducing anxiety and improving mental health.

3. Better Time Management:

- Scheduled Study Sessions: Consistency allows for scheduled study sessions, making it easier to balance studies with other commitments.

- Avoid Procrastination: Regular study habits reduce the temptation to procrastinate, ensuring steady progress.

4. Enhanced Focus and Concentration:

- Daily Practice: Regular study sessions help in developing better focus and concentration over time.

- Minimize Burnout: Intense study sessions can lead to fatigue and burnout, while consistent study keeps you energized and engaged.

5. Builds Discipline and Habit:

- Routine Formation: Consistent study helps in forming strong study habits and discipline, which are essential for CA preparation.

- Accountability: Regular study schedules hold you accountable, helping you stay on track with your goals.

Practical Tips for Consistency:

1. Set Realistic Goals: Break down your syllabus into daily or weekly goals that are achievable and realistic.

2. Create a Study Schedule: Plan your study sessions in advance and stick to the schedule. Consistency in timing helps in forming a habit.

3. Regular Breaks: Incorporate short breaks to avoid burnout and maintain productivity.

4. Stay Organized: Keep your study materials organized and readily available to make the most of your study time.

5. Self-Motivation: Keep reminding yourself of your long-term goals and the importance of daily efforts.

By focusing on consistency, CA students can achieve steady progress, reduce stress, and build a strong foundation for their exams. Remember, small, consistent efforts lead to big achievements! ???

CHAPTER SIXTY-NINE

FINDING CLARITY IN UNCERTAINTY: NAVIGATING THE FOGGY PATH

Imagine you are hiking up a mountain trail early in the morning. The path ahead is shrouded in dense fog, making it difficult to see more than a few steps in front of you. You know the destination is a beautiful summit with breathtaking views, but the journey seems uncertain and daunting.

Despite the fog, you decide to move forward. Each step you take reveals a bit more of the path. Occasionally, you encounter obstacles like rocks and branches, but you navigate around them. Every so often, the fog clears slightly, giving you a glimpse of the trail ahead and boosting your confidence to keep going.

As you continue, you learn to trust the process, using your intuition and experience to guide you. You rely on markers and signs along the way, reminding yourself of the direction. Gradually, the fog begins to lift, and the path becomes clearer. Finally, after persistent effort, you reach the summit, rewarded with a magnificent view and a profound sense of accomplishment.

Lessons for CA Students

1. Start Moving Forward:

- Even when the path isn't entirely clear, taking the first step is crucial. Begin your studies with what you know and gradually expand your knowledge.

2. Trust the Process:

- Trust that your efforts will lead to clarity. Study consistently, and over time, the concepts will become clearer.

3. Learn from Obstacles:

- Challenges are part of the journey. Each obstacle you overcome adds to your experience and knowledge.

4. Use Resources:

- Like the trail markers, use study guides, mentors, and resources to stay on the right track.

5. Gradual Clarity:

- Understanding comes with time. Don't rush the process; clarity will emerge as you persist.

6. Celebrate Milestones:

- Each small clearing in the fog is a milestone. Celebrate your progress to stay motivated.

7. Stay Persistent:

- Keep moving forward, even when the way seems unclear. Persistence is key to reaching your goal.

Applying the Story to CA Studies

- Begin with Small Steps: Start your study sessions with manageable goals. Over time, increase the complexity.

- Trust Your Study Plan: Follow a structured study plan and trust that your efforts will pay off.

- Overcome Challenges: When you encounter difficult topics, tackle them head-on and learn from them.

- Use Study Resources: Utilize textbooks, online resources, and peer discussions to guide your learning.

- Celebrate Progress: Acknowledge and celebrate each topic you master and each exam you pass.

- Stay Persistent: Keep your end goal in sight and stay motivated, even when progress seems slow.

By embracing the journey through the fog, CA students can find clarity and achieve their goals. Every step you take brings you closer to the summit of your success.

CHAPTER SEVENTY

FINDING STRENGTH IN ADVERSITY: OVERCOMING DIFFICULT PROBLEMS

Handling difficult problems or hurdles requires resilience, determination, and a positive mindset. When faced with obstacles, viewing them as opportunities for growth and learning can make a significant difference. Embracing challenges head-on and breaking them down into manageable steps can make them less daunting. Developing strategies to navigate tough terrains helps build resilience and adaptability. Whether it's through seeking support, staying focused, or maintaining a positive attitude, transforming obstacles into achievements becomes possible. By turning trials into triumphs and viewing hurdles as stepping stones, we can thrive amidst adversity and find strength in overcoming life's toughest problems.

Handling difficult problems and hurdles is an integral part of the journey for CA students. Here are some strategies to help you navigate through these challenges:

1. Break Down the Problem

- Simplify: Divide complex problems into smaller, more manageable parts. Tackle each part one at a time.

- Prioritize: Focus on the most crucial aspects first. This helps in making progress and reduces the overwhelming feeling.

2. Stay Organized

- Create a Plan: Develop a clear study plan with specific goals and deadlines.

- Use Tools: Utilize planners, apps, or spreadsheets to keep track of your progress and stay organized.

3. Seek Help

- Ask for Guidance: Don't hesitate to seek help from mentors, teachers, or peers. Collaborative learning can provide new insights and solutions.

- Study Groups: Join or form study groups where you can discuss and solve problems together.

4. Practice Resilience

- Stay Positive: Maintain a positive attitude even when faced with setbacks. Believe in your ability to overcome challenges.

- Learn from Mistakes: View mistakes as learning opportunities. Analyze what went wrong and use that knowledge to improve.

5. Use Resources

- Study Material: Make the most of available study materials, including textbooks, online resources, and past exam papers.

- Professional Help: Consider enrolling in coaching classes or online courses for additional support.

6. Time Management

- Set Priorities: Allocate your time wisely between different subjects and tasks.

- Avoid Procrastination: Stick to your study schedule and avoid putting off difficult topics.

7. Stay Healthy

- Physical Health: Ensure you get enough rest, eat healthy, and exercise regularly.

- Mental Health: Practice stress-relief techniques like meditation, deep breathing, or taking short breaks during study sessions.

8. Develop Problem-Solving Skills

- Critical Thinking: Enhance your critical thinking skills by questioning assumptions, analyzing information, and considering multiple solutions.

- Practice, Practice, Practice: Solve as many practice questions and past papers as you can to build confidence and proficiency.

9. Stay Motivated

- Set Achievable Goals: Keep setting and achieving short-term goals to stay motivated.

- Reward Yourself: Treat yourself for small victories to keep morale high.

10. Adaptability

- Flexible Approach: Be open to adjusting your study methods if something isn't working. Adaptability is key to overcoming hurdles.

Remember, every challenge you overcome brings you one step closer to your goal. Stay persistent, believe in your abilities, and keep moving forward. You've got what it takes to succeed! ?

CHAPTER SEVENTY-ONE

DIVIDE AND CONQUER: TACKLING CHALLENGES BY DEBUNDLING THE PROBLEM.

In the world of Chartered Accountancy (CA), students often face complex problems that can seem overwhelming. However, adopting the "divide and conquer" approach can make even the most daunting challenges more manageable. This method involves breaking down a problem into smaller, more manageable parts, addressing each part individually, and ultimately solving the larger issue through these incremental steps. The classic story of the bundle of sticks provides a powerful analogy for this approach.

The Story of the Bundle of Sticks

Once upon a time, there was an old man with several sons who were always quarreling among themselves. To teach them a lesson, the old man called his sons together and handed each of them a stick. He asked them to break the sticks, which they easily did. Then, he tied the sticks together into a bundle and handed it to his sons, asking them to break the bundle. Try as they might, the sons could not break the bundle of sticks.

The old man then untied the bundle and handed the sticks to his sons one by one, and they were able to break each stick with ease. He explained, "My sons, if you are united like this bundle, no one can harm you. But if you are divided, you will be broken as easily as these individual sticks."

In the world of Chartered Accountancy (CA), students often face complex problems that can seem overwhelming. However, adopting the "divide and conquer" approach can make even the most daunting challenges more manageable. This method involves breaking down a problem into smaller, more manageable parts, addressing each part individually, and ultimately solving the larger issue through these incremental steps. The classic story of the bundle of sticks provides a powerful analogy for this approach.

The Story of the Bundle of Sticks

Once upon a time, there was an old man with several sons who were always quarreling among themselves. To teach them a lesson, the old man called his sons together and handed each of them a stick. He asked them to break the sticks, which they easily did. Then, he tied the sticks together into a bundle and handed it to his sons, asking them to break the bundle. Try as they might, the sons could not break the bundle of sticks.

The old man then untied the bundle and handed the sticks to his sons one by one, and they were able to break each stick with ease. He explained, "My sons, if you are united like this bundle, no one can harm you. But if you are divided, you will be broken as easily as these individual sticks."

Applying the Lesson to CA Studies

The lesson from the bundle of sticks is directly applicable to the challenges CA students face. Complex problems in accounting, taxation, and financial management can be overwhelming when viewed as a whole. However, by "debundling" these problems and addressing each component individually, students can effectively manage and conquer their challenges.

For CA students, complex problems can often feel like an unbreakable bundle of sticks. Here's how you can apply the lesson:

1. Identify Sub-Tasks: Break down the complex problem into smaller, manageable parts or sub-tasks. Just like breaking the bundle into individual sticks.

2. Tackle One by One: Focus on solving each smaller part one at a time. This makes the problem less overwhelming and more manageable.

3. Build Confidence: Solving smaller problems step by step builds your confidence and momentum, making it easier to tackle the entire problem.

4. Stay Organized: Keep track of your progress and ensure that each sub-task contributes to the overall solution.

Example for CA Students

Suppose you are preparing for the topic of "Consolidated Financial Statements":

- Break Down the Topic: Divide it into sub-topics like understanding the concepts of parent-subsidiary relationships, accounting for investments, inter-company transactions, and preparation of consolidated balance sheets.

- Study Each Sub-Topic: Focus on each sub-topic individually. Study the theory, solve practical problems, and understand the nuances.

- Integrate Knowledge: Once you've mastered each sub-topic, integrate them to understand the full picture of consolidated financial statements.

By breaking down complex problems into smaller, more manageable parts, you can handle them more effectively and reduce the feeling of being overwhelmed. Remember, every step forward, no matter how small, brings you closer to mastering the material and succeeding in your exams.

The story of the bundle of sticks teaches us the importance of unity and collaboration. For CA students, this lesson can be applied by "debundling" complex problems and addressing each part individually. By breaking down challenges, prioritizing tasks, leveraging resources, maintaining consistency, celebrating small wins, and reflecting on the process, students can effectively tackle even the most complex issues. Remember, no problem is insurmountable when approached with the right strategy and mindset. Embrace the "divide and conquer" approach, and you will find that the path to success becomes much clearer and more attainable.

The lesson from the bundle of sticks is directly applicable to the challenges CA students face. Complex problems in accounting, taxation, and financial management can be overwhelming when viewed as a whole. However, by "debundling" these problems and addressing each component individually, students can effectively manage and conquer their challenges.

For CA students, complex problems can often feel like an unbreakable bundle of sticks. Here's how you can apply the lesson:

1. Identify Sub-Tasks: Break down the complex problem into smaller, manageable parts or sub-tasks. Just like breaking the bundle into individual sticks.

2. Tackle One by One: Focus on solving each smaller part one at a time. This makes the problem less overwhelming and more manageable.

3. Build Confidence: Solving smaller problems step by step builds your confidence and momentum, making it easier to tackle the entire problem.

4. Stay Organized: Keep track of your progress and ensure that each sub-task contributes to the overall solution.

Example for CA Students

Suppose you are preparing for the topic of "Consolidated Financial Statements":

- Break Down the Topic: Divide it into sub-topics like understanding the concepts of parent-subsidiary relationships, accounting for investments, inter-company transactions, and preparation of consolidated balance sheets.

- Study Each Sub-Topic: Focus on each sub-topic individually. Study the theory, solve practical problems, and understand the nuances.

- Integrate Knowledge: Once you've mastered each sub-topic, integrate them to understand the full picture of consolidated financial statements.

By breaking down complex problems into smaller, more manageable parts, you can handle them more effectively and reduce the feeling of being overwhelmed. Remember, every step forward, no matter how small, brings you closer to mastering the material and succeeding in your exams.

The story of the bundle of sticks teaches us the importance of unity and collaboration. For CA students, this lesson can be applied by "debundling" complex problems and addressing each part individually. By breaking down challenges, prioritizing tasks, leveraging resources, maintaining consistency, celebrating small wins, and reflecting on the process, students can effectively tackle even the most complex issues. Remember, no problem is insurmountable when approached with the right strategy and mindset. Embrace the "divide and conquer" approach, and you will find that the path to success becomes much clearer and more attainable.

CHAPTER SEVENTY-TWO

AVOIDING DISTRACTIONS AND STAYING FOCUSED

Avoiding distractions is crucial for CA students to maintain focus and productivity. Here are some effective strategies to help you stay on track:

Strategies to Avoid Distractions

1. Create a Dedicated Study Space:

- Designate a specific area for studying that is free from distractions like TV, household noise, and other activities. Keep this space tidy and organized.

2. Set Clear Boundaries:

- Inform family and roommates of your study schedule so they can minimize interruptions. Use a "Do Not Disturb" sign if necessary.

3. Limit Digital Distractions:

- Turn off notifications on your phone, tablet, and computer. Use apps like "Focus@Will" or website blockers like "StayFocusd" to block distracting websites and apps during study sessions.

4. Follow a Study Schedule:

- Create a study timetable and stick to it. Having a structured plan can help you stay focused and make the most of your study time.

5. Use the Time Blocking Technique:

- Study in short, focused bursts (e.g., 25 minutes) followed by a short break (e.g., 5 minutes). This method helps maintain concentration and gives your mind regular rest periods.

6. Break Tasks into Smaller Steps:

- Divide large tasks into smaller, manageable steps. This makes them less daunting and helps you stay focused on completing one step at a time.

7. Mindfulness and Meditation:

- Practice mindfulness or meditation to improve your concentration and reduce the tendency to get distracted. Even a few minutes of deep breathing can help.

8. Healthy Snacks and Hydration:

- Keep healthy snacks and water nearby to prevent unnecessary trips to the kitchen, which can break your focus.

9. Regular Breaks:

- Take regular breaks to rest and recharge. Use this time to stretch, walk, or do something relaxing. Avoid screen time during breaks to give your eyes a rest.

10. Reward System:

- Set up a reward system for yourself. After completing a study session or a specific task, reward yourself with a small treat or a break to do something you enjoy.

11. Stay Organized:

- Keep your study materials and notes organized. Use folders, binders, and digital tools to keep track of your progress and avoid wasting time looking for materials.

By implementing these strategies, you can minimize distractions and create a focused study environment that enhances your productivity. Keep up the good work! ?

CHAPTER SEVENTY-THREE

THE STORY OF ARJUNA'S FOCUS

During their training under Guru Dronacharya, the Kauravas and Pandavas were given an archery test. Dronacharya placed a wooden bird on a tree and asked his students to aim at its eye. Before allowing them to shoot, he asked each one what they saw.

- Yudhishthira: "I see the bird, the tree, and the sky."

- Bhima: "I see the bird and the tree."

- Duryodhana: "I see the bird and the leaves around it."

When it was Arjuna's turn, he replied, "I see only the eye of the bird." Pleased with his answer, Dronacharya allowed him to shoot, and Arjuna hit the bird's eye perfectly.

Lessons for CA Students

1. Single-minded Focus:

- Just as Arjuna focused solely on the bird's eye, CA students should focus intently on their studies, blocking out distractions.

2. Clear Vision:

- Have a clear vision of your goals. Know what you want to achieve and direct all your efforts toward it.

3. Prioritize:

- Focus on what is most important. Prioritize key topics and subjects that need more attention.

4. Discipline:

- Maintain a disciplined study routine. Consistency and discipline are key to mastering your subjects.

5. Minimize Distractions:

- Create a study environment free from distractions. Limit social media and other interruptions during study time.

Practical Applications

1. Set Specific Goals: Break down your study material into specific, manageable goals.

2. Daily Targets: Set daily targets and strive to achieve them.

3. Focused Study Sessions: Use techniques like the Pomodoro Technique to maintain focus during study sessions.

4. Visualization: Visualize your goals and keep them in mind to stay motivated.

5. Mindfulness and Meditation: Practice mindfulness or meditation to improve concentration and reduce stress.

By channeling Arjuna's unwavering focus and determination, you can enhance your study habits and achieve your CA goals. Stay focused on your "bird's eye" and aim with precision!

CHAPTER SEVENTY-FOUR

THE STORY OF THE HORSE AND THE BLINDER

A farmer owned a hardworking horse that he used to plow his fields. To ensure the horse stayed focused on the task at hand, the farmer fitted it with blinders. These blinders, or eye masks, covered the sides of the horse's eyes, limiting its field of vision. With these on, the horse couldn't see distractions around it and could only look straight ahead at its path.

By wearing the blinders, the horse was able to concentrate solely on plowing the field, without being startled or distracted by movements or noises in its peripheral vision. As a result, the work was done more efficiently and quickly.

Lessons for CA Students

1. Stay Focused

- Just like the horse with blinders, CA students should focus on their studies and block out distractions. This means creating a conducive study environment, free from interruptions.

2. Limit Distractions

- Identify and minimize distractions that can divert your attention from studying. This could be as simple as turning off notifications on your phone, finding a quiet study space, or setting specific times for breaks.

3. Set Clear Goals

- Having clear goals helps in maintaining focus. Know what you need to achieve in each study session and keep your eyes on those targets.

4. Follow a Routine

- Establishing a consistent study routine can help in developing discipline and making it easier to stay focused. A routine trains your mind to switch into study mode at specific times.

5. Use Tools and Techniques

- Utilize study aids like planners, timers, and apps that can help you stay organized and focused. Techniques like the Pomodoro Technique can be particularly effective in maintaining concentration.

Applying the Story to Your CA Journey

1. Create a Focused Study Environment: Find or create a space dedicated to studying where you can minimize distractions.

2. Set Specific Study Goals: Define what you want to accomplish in each study session and work towards those goals.

3. Establish a Routine: Develop a regular study schedule that includes breaks to ensure you don't burn out.

4. Use Blinders for Your Mind: Just as the horse's blinders help it focus, use mental blinders by avoiding multitasking and keeping your study sessions distraction-free.

5. Track Your Progress: Regularly review your progress and adjust your strategies as needed to stay on track.

By adopting the lessons from the story of the horse and the eye mask, CA students can enhance their focus, reduce distractions, and improve their efficiency and productivity in their studies. ??

CHAPTER SEVENTY-FIVE

Tips to Avoid Social Media Distractions

Social media can be a significant distraction for CA students, but with some discipline and strategies, you can manage and minimize these distractions. Here are some tips to help you stay focused:

1. Set Clear Goals and Priorities:

- Define your study goals and priorities clearly. Having a clear understanding of what you need to accomplish can help you stay focused.

2. Create a Study Schedule:

- Develop a detailed study schedule that includes specific time slots for studying and breaks. Stick to this schedule to maintain a routine.

3. Limit Access:

- Use apps or tools that block social media websites during study hours. Apps like Freedom, StayFocusd, and Cold Turkey can help limit your access to distracting sites.

- Temporarily disable notifications on your devices or use the "Do Not Disturb" mode while studying.

4. Designate Specific Times for Social Media:

- Allocate specific times during the day for checking social media. This can be during your breaks or after you've completed your study goals for the day.

5. Use Social Media Wisely:

- Turn off unnecessary notifications and only keep essential ones.

- Unfollow or mute accounts that are not related to your studies or that you find distracting.

6. Study Environment:

- Create a dedicated and distraction-free study space. Keep your phone or other devices out of reach while studying.

7. Accountability:

- Share your study goals and progress with a friend or family member who can help keep you accountable.

- Join study groups or forums where you can discuss your progress and challenges with peers.

8. Mindfulness and Focus Techniques:

- Practice mindfulness or meditation to improve your concentration and reduce the urge to check social media.

- Use techniques like the Pomodoro Technique to break your study sessions into focused intervals with short breaks in between.

9. Reward System:

- Set up a reward system for yourself. For example, allow yourself a few minutes on social media only after completing a certain amount of study.

10. Self-Reflection:

- Regularly reflect on your use of social media and its impact on your studies. Make adjustments to your habits as needed to ensure you stay focused.

By implementing these strategies, you can manage social media distractions and maintain your focus on your CA exam preparation. Good luck, and stay disciplined! ???

CHAPTER SEVENTY-SIX

DEVELOPING STRONG WRITING SKILLS IS ESSENTIAL FOR CA STUDENTS

Developing strong writing skills is essential for CA students, as it helps in clear communication of complex ideas, structured answers, and effective presentation during exams. Here are some tips to enhance your writing skills:

Tips for Improving Writing Skills

1. Understand the Question:

- Read Carefully: Ensure you fully understand what the question is asking. Look for keywords that indicate the required response, such as "explain," "compare," "analyze," or "describe."

- Outline Your Answer: Plan your response before you start writing. Create a brief outline to organize your thoughts and ensure a logical flow.

2. Use Clear and Concise Language:

- Avoid Jargon: Use simple and clear language. Avoid unnecessary jargon and complex words unless they are relevant to the subject.

- Be Direct: Get straight to the point. Avoid long-winded introductions and focus on delivering your main ideas concisely.

3. Structure Your Answer:

- Introduction: Start with a brief introduction that outlines the main points you will cover.

- Body: Divide the main content into clear, logical sections or paragraphs. Use headings and subheadings if necessary.

- Conclusion: Summarize the key points and reiterate the main conclusion or answer to the question.

4. Practice Grammar and Punctuation:

- Correct Usage: Ensure your grammar and punctuation are correct. This improves the readability of your work and conveys professionalism.

- Proofread: Always proofread your answers to catch any grammatical or typographical errors.

5. Use Examples and Illustrations:

- Relevant Examples: Use relevant examples, case studies, and illustrations to support your arguments and explanations.

- Visual Aids: Incorporate diagrams, charts, and tables where appropriate to make your answers more comprehensive and easier to understand.

6. Stay Objective and Neutral:

- Balanced Perspective: Present a balanced perspective, especially in discussions or analyses. Avoid letting personal biases influence your writing.

- Cite Sources: Where applicable, reference relevant laws, standards, or authoritative texts to support your points.

7. Practice Past Papers:

- Mock Exams: Regularly practice writing answers to past exam questions under timed conditions. This helps you get used to the exam format and improves your time management.

- Feedback: Seek feedback on your practice answers from mentors or peers to identify areas for improvement.

8. Enhance Your Vocabulary:

- Read Widely: Read articles, books, and reports related to accountancy and finance. This not only improves your vocabulary but also keeps you updated with industry trends.

- Use a Thesaurus: Use a thesaurus to find synonyms and expand your word choice, but ensure the words you choose are appropriate for the context.

9. Engage in Peer Review:

- Study Groups: Participate in study groups where you can exchange written work and provide constructive feedback to each other.

- Peer Review: Reviewing others' work can help you gain new perspectives and improve your own writing.

Example of Structured Writing:

Question: Explain the significance of internal controls in an organization.

Answer:

Introduction:

Internal controls are mechanisms, policies, and procedures implemented by an organization to ensure the integrity of financial and accounting information, promote accountability, and prevent fraud.

Body:

1. Safeguarding Assets:

Internal controls help protect the organization's assets from theft, loss, or misuse. For instance, regular audits and inventory checks can detect discrepancies and prevent asset misappropriation.

2. Ensuring Accuracy:

These controls ensure that financial records are accurate and reliable. Examples include reconciliation of accounts, segregation of duties, and authorization procedures.

3. Promoting Efficiency:

Internal controls streamline operations by defining standard procedures, which minimize errors and enhance efficiency. For example, automated approval workflows reduce the time taken for transaction approvals.

4. Compliance with Laws:

Organizations must comply with various laws and regulations. Internal controls help ensure compliance, such as adherence to tax regulations and industry standards.

Conclusion:

In conclusion, internal controls are vital for safeguarding assets, ensuring the accuracy of financial records, promoting operational efficiency, and maintaining compliance with laws and regulations. Implementing robust internal controls is essential for the overall health and sustainability of an organization.

By incorporating these tips and practicing regularly, you can enhance your writing skills and perform better in your CA exams. Keep writing, and best of luck with your studies!

CHAPTER SEVENTY-SEVEN

How to Wake Up on Time Without an Alarm

Waking up on time without an alarm involves establishing a consistent routine, optimizing your sleep environment, and using mental preparation techniques. Here's how you can rise and shine naturally:

1. Maintain a Consistent Sleep Schedule

- Regular Bedtime: Go to bed and wake up at the same time every day, even on weekends. This helps regulate your internal clock.

- Gradual Adjustments: If you need to change your sleep schedule, do it gradually by adjusting your bedtime and wake-up time by 15 minutes each day.

2. Create a Bedtime Routine

- Relaxing Activities: Engage in calming activities before bed, such as reading, meditating, or taking a warm bath.

- Limit Screen Time: Avoid screens at least an hour before bed to reduce blue light exposure, which can interfere with sleep.

3. Optimize Your Sleep Environment

- Comfortable Bedding: Ensure your mattress and pillows are comfortable and supportive.

- Dark and Cool Room: Keep your bedroom dark and cool to promote better sleep. Consider blackout curtains and a cool temperature.

4. Natural Light Exposure

- Morning Sunlight: Expose yourself to natural light in the morning. Open the curtains as soon as you wake up or spend some time outside.

- Daytime Light: Try to get plenty of natural light during the day to help regulate your circadian rhythm.

5. Healthy Lifestyle Habits

- Exercise Regularly: Engage in regular physical activity, but avoid vigorous exercise close to bedtime.

- Limit Caffeine and Heavy Meals: Avoid caffeine and large meals close to bedtime as they can disrupt your sleep.

6. Mental Preparation and Subconscious Instruction

- Set Your Intention: Before going to bed, clearly set your intention to wake up at a specific time. Visualize yourself waking up feeling refreshed and ready to start the day.

- Positive Affirmations: Repeat positive affirmations such as "I will wake up at 6 AM feeling energized and alert." This helps program your subconscious mind.

- Visualization: Imagine yourself waking up at the desired time. Visualize the sequence of events: hearing the morning sounds, seeing the light, and feeling the sensation of waking up naturally.

7. Use Gentle Cues

- Natural Wake-Up Light: If you need some assistance, consider using a wake-up light that simulates a natural sunrise to gently wake you.

Practice and Patience

Establishing these habits takes time and consistency. Be patient with yourself as your body adjusts to a natural wake-up routine.

By following these tips, you'll be well on your way to waking up on time without the need for an alarm. Sweet dreams and bright mornings ahead!

CHAPTER SEVENTY-EIGHT

TIME MANAGEMENT FOR SUCCESS

In a lush forest, a wise old owl named Oliver shared a valuable lesson on time management with a young rabbit named Rosie. Rosie struggled to prepare for the changing seasons, but Oliver recounted the story of Sam the squirrel, who learned from hardworking ants to plan and prepare in advance. Inspired by this tale, Rosie started gathering food and building a shelter early, ensuring she was ready for the colder months. This experience taught her the importance of foresight and consistent effort, helping her face future challenges with confidence and readiness.

In the demanding field of Chartered Accountancy, effective time management is crucial for success. The story of Rosie the rabbit and the wise owl, Oliver, serves as a valuable lesson. Just as Rosie struggled to prepare for the changing seasons, CA students often face the challenge of balancing rigorous studies, exams, and practical training. By learning from the story, CA students can see the importance of planning and preparing in advance.

Just as Rosie was inspired by the tale of Sam the squirrel, who learned from the ants to work steadily and avoid last-minute rushes, CA students can benefit from breaking down their tasks into manageable parts and creating a study schedule. Prioritizing tasks, setting realistic goals, and maintaining consistency are key. By managing time wisely, students can reduce stress, improve productivity, and achieve a balanced lifestyle.

Time management is not just about working hard but also about working smart. Incorporating regular breaks and ensuring a healthy work-life balance can enhance focus and efficiency. The story reminds us that with proper planning and time management, CA students can tackle their academic and professional challenges with confidence and readiness, ultimately leading to success in their careers.

Implementing these strategies can help you manage your time effectively, reduce stress, and ensure comprehensive preparation for your CA exams. Remember, consistency and discipline are key to success!

CHAPTER SEVENTY-NINE

IMPORTANCE OF EXERCISE

Exercise is crucial for CA students, given the high level of mental exertion and long hours of study involved. Here's why incorporating physical activity into your routine can be immensely beneficial:

Importance of Exercise for CA Students

1. Improves Cognitive Function:

- Exercise increases blood flow to the brain, enhancing cognitive functions like memory, concentration, and problem-solving skills, which are vital for tackling complex subjects in CA.

2. Reduces Stress and Anxiety:

- Physical activity releases endorphins, which are natural mood lifters. It helps in reducing stress and anxiety, promoting a calm and focused mind essential for effective studying.

3. Boosts Energy Levels:

- Regular exercise improves overall energy levels and combats fatigue. This means you can study longer and more effectively without feeling drained.

4. Improves Sleep Quality:

- Better sleep is crucial for memory consolidation and cognitive function. Exercise helps regulate sleep patterns, ensuring you get quality rest to rejuvenate your mind and body.

5. Enhances Physical Health:

- Staying active helps prevent health issues like back pain, which is common among students who sit for extended periods. It also improves cardiovascular health, stamina, and overall fitness.

6. Improves Mood and Motivation:

- Exercise stimulates the production of chemicals that help you feel happier and more relaxed. This positive outlook can significantly enhance your motivation and perseverance in your studies.

7. Promotes Better Time Management:

- Including regular exercise in your daily schedule teaches discipline and time management. Balancing study sessions with physical activity can lead to more efficient use of time.

8. Increases Social Interaction:

- Engaging in group sports or fitness classes can increase your social interactions, reducing feelings of isolation and promoting a balanced, healthy lifestyle.

Practical Tips for Incorporating Exercise:

- Short Breaks: Take short breaks between study sessions to do quick exercises like stretching, jumping jacks, or a brisk walk.

- Morning Routine: Start your day with a workout to boost your energy and set a positive tone for the day.

- Join Classes: Enroll in fitness classes or sports activities to stay motivated and committed.

- Home Workouts: Use online resources or fitness apps for guided home workouts that fit into your schedule.

- Study and Exercise: Consider active studying methods, like walking while reading notes or listening to recorded lectures.

By making exercise a regular part of your routine, you can significantly enhance your physical and mental well-being, ultimately supporting your academic performance. Stay active and thrive!

CHAPTER EIGHTY

IMPORTANCE OF A HEALTHY DIET

Our bodies are a reflection of the food we consume, making it crucial to prioritize healthy eating. Nutritious foods provide the essential vitamins, minerals, and nutrients our bodies need to function optimally. A balanced diet rich in fruits, vegetables, whole grains, lean proteins, and healthy fats can boost our immune system, enhance energy levels, and support overall well-being. Moreover, a nutritious diet can improve mental clarity, mood, and cognitive function, contributing to a more productive and fulfilling life. By making mindful food choices, we can ensure that our bodies are well-nourished and capable of performing at their best.

Maintaining a healthy diet is vital for CA students, who often face long hours of study and high levels of mental stress. Here are some reasons why a balanced diet is crucial:

Importance of a Healthy Diet for CA Students

1. Boosts Brain Function:

- Nutrient-rich foods like fruits, vegetables, nuts, and fish contain essential vitamins, minerals, and omega-3 fatty acids that enhance brain function, memory, and cognitive skills.

2. Increases Energy Levels:

- A balanced diet provides the necessary nutrients to keep energy levels stable throughout the day. Foods high in protein, healthy fats, and complex carbohydrates help maintain energy and prevent fatigue.

3. Enhances Concentration:

- Consuming a variety of foods ensures a steady supply of glucose to the brain, which is essential for concentration and focus during long study sessions.

4. Reduces Stress:

- Foods rich in antioxidants, vitamins, and minerals, such as berries, leafy greens, and whole grains, can help reduce oxidative stress and improve overall well-being.

5. Supports Physical Health:

- A balanced diet helps maintain a healthy weight, supports immune function, and reduces the risk of chronic diseases, which can be particularly important during periods of intense study.

6. Improves Sleep Quality:

- Proper nutrition can influence sleep patterns and quality. Foods high in magnesium, like nuts and seeds, can help promote relaxation and better sleep.

7. Enhances Mood:

- A healthy diet rich in whole foods, lean proteins, and complex carbohydrates can stabilize mood and reduce symptoms of anxiety and depression, which are common during exam preparation.

Practical Dietary Tips for CA Students

- Breakfast: Start your day with a balanced breakfast, including protein, whole grains, and fruits. For example, oatmeal with berries and nuts or a smoothie with spinach, banana, and yogurt.

- Stay Hydrated: Drink plenty of water throughout the day to stay hydrated. Dehydration can impair cognitive function and concentration.

- Healthy Snacks: Choose healthy snacks like fruits, nuts, yogurt, or whole-grain crackers to keep your energy levels up between meals.

- Balanced Meals: Aim for meals that include a variety of nutrients. Include lean proteins (chicken, fish, tofu), whole grains (brown rice, quinoa), and plenty of vegetables.

- Limit Processed Foods: Avoid excessive consumption of processed and sugary foods, which can lead to energy crashes and affect your focus.

- Plan and Prep: Plan your meals and prepare healthy options in advance to avoid resorting to unhealthy fast food during busy study periods.

By prioritizing a nutritious and balanced diet, CA students can significantly improve their physical and mental health, enhancing their ability to study effectively and succeed in their exams. Stay healthy and keep thriving!

CHAPTER EIGHTY-ONE

IMPORTANCE OF SLEEP

Sleep is a crucial component for CA students, particularly given the demanding nature of their studies. Here are several reasons why getting adequate rest is vital:

Importance of Sleep for CA Students

1. Enhances Memory and Learning:

- Sleep plays a key role in consolidating memories and processing information. This is essential for retaining the complex material that CA students study.

2. Improves Cognitive Function:

- Adequate sleep is linked to better concentration, problem-solving skills, and decision-making abilities, which are crucial for effective studying and exam performance.

3. Boosts Mood and Mental Health:

- Good sleep helps regulate mood and reduce stress. Poor sleep can lead to increased anxiety and depression, which can negatively impact studying and overall well-being.

4. Increases Energy Levels:

- Restful sleep replenishes energy stores, allowing students to stay alert and focused throughout the day.

5. Supports Physical Health:

- Sleep is essential for maintaining a healthy immune system, reducing the risk of illnesses that could disrupt study schedules.

6. Enhances Productivity:

- Well-rested students can work more efficiently, making the most of their study time and maintaining better productivity.

Practical Tips for Better Sleep

- Stick to a Schedule: Go to bed and wake up at the same time every day, even on weekends, to regulate your sleep cycle.

- Create a Sleep-Friendly Environment: Ensure your bedroom is dark, quiet, and cool. Consider using earplugs, eye masks, or white noise machines if needed.

- Limit Screen Time: Avoid screens (phones, tablets, laptops) at least an hour before bedtime, as the blue light can interfere with melatonin production.

- Relax Before Bed: Develop a pre-sleep routine to help unwind. This could include reading, listening to calming music, or practicing relaxation techniques.

- Watch Your Diet: Avoid heavy meals, caffeine, and alcohol close to bedtime, as they can disrupt sleep.

- Stay Active: Regular physical activity can help you fall asleep faster and enjoy deeper sleep. Just avoid vigorous exercise right before bed.

- Manage Stress: Incorporate stress-reduction techniques like meditation, yoga, or journaling into your daily routine to improve sleep quality.

By prioritizing sleep, CA students can enhance their cognitive functions, emotional well-being, and overall performance, leading to better academic success and a healthier lifestyle. Sleep tight and study smart! ???

CHAPTER EIGHTY-TWO

MIND MANAGEMENT TECHNIQUES FOR CA STUDENTS

Mind management is essential for CA students to maintain focus, reduce stress, and enhance productivity. Here are some effective strategies to help you manage your mind while navigating the rigorous CA curriculum:

Mind Management Techniques for CA Students

1. Set Clear Goals:

- Define specific, achievable goals for your studies. Break down large tasks into smaller, manageable steps to avoid feeling overwhelmed.

2. Create a Study Schedule:

- Plan your study sessions in advance, allocating time for each subject based on your priorities and deadlines. Stick to the schedule to maintain a steady pace.

3. Practice Mindfulness:

- Incorporate mindfulness techniques such as meditation, deep breathing exercises, or yoga into your daily routine. These practices can help reduce stress and improve focus.

4. Stay Organized:

- Keep your study materials and workspace organized. Use tools like planners, to-do lists, and digital apps to track your progress and deadlines.

5. Limit Distractions:

- Identify and minimize distractions in your study environment. This could include turning off notifications, setting specific study times, and creating a quiet, dedicated workspace.

6. Take Regular Breaks:

- Avoid long, continuous study sessions. Use the Pomodoro Technique or similar methods to take short breaks between study intervals to rejuvenate your mind.

7. Exercise Regularly:

- Physical activity can help clear your mind, reduce stress, and boost overall well-being. Aim for at least 30 minutes of exercise daily.

8. Stay Positive:

- Maintain a positive mindset and practice self-compassion. Acknowledge your progress and celebrate small victories to stay motivated.

9. Practice Active Learning:

- Engage with the material actively by taking notes, asking questions, discussing with peers, and teaching others. Active learning enhances understanding and retention.

10. Seek Support:

- Don't hesitate to seek help from mentors, peers, or professional counselors if you feel overwhelmed. Support systems are crucial for mental well-being.

By integrating these mind management strategies into your routine, you can enhance your focus, reduce stress, and achieve a balanced and productive study experience. Keep up the great work!

CHAPTER EIGHTY-THREE

STRATEGIES FOR EMOTION MANAGEMENT

Managing emotions is critical for CA students given the intense pressure and demanding nature of the course. Here are some strategies to help you manage your emotions effectively:

Strategies for Emotion Management

1. Recognize and Acknowledge Emotions:

- Understand and accept your emotions instead of suppressing them. Recognizing how you feel is the first step towards managing it.

2. Practice Mindfulness and Meditation:

- Mindfulness practices, such as meditation and deep breathing exercises, can help you stay grounded and calm. Just a few minutes each day can make a significant difference.

3. Maintain a Healthy Lifestyle:

- Ensure you get adequate sleep, eat a balanced diet, and exercise regularly. Physical health has a direct impact on emotional well-being.

4. Set Realistic Goals:

- Break your study goals into manageable tasks and set realistic expectations. This reduces the risk of feeling overwhelmed and stressed.

5. Develop a Support System:

- Surround yourself with supportive friends, family, and peers. Don't hesitate to reach out to them when you're feeling down or stressed.

6. Take Regular Breaks:

- Incorporate short breaks into your study routine to relax and recharge. Use this time to do something you enjoy, like listening to music, reading, or going for a walk.

7. Positive Self-Talk:

- Practice positive affirmations and self-talk. Replace negative thoughts with encouraging and constructive ones.

8. Journaling:

- Keep a journal to write down your thoughts and feelings. This can help you process emotions and reflect on your experiences.

9. Seek Professional Help:

- If you're struggling with intense emotions or persistent stress, consider talking to a counselor or therapist. They can provide professional guidance and support.

10. Engage in Hobbies:

- Make time for activities and hobbies you enjoy. Engaging in creative or recreational activities can be a great way to manage stress and improve your mood.

By incorporating these emotion management strategies into your daily routine, you can enhance your resilience, stay positive, and maintain a healthy balance between your studies and personal well-being. Remember, taking care of your emotional health is just as important as your academic success.

CHAPTER EIGHTY-FOUR

STRESS MANAGEMENT TECHNIQUES

Managing stress is essential for CA students to maintain focus, productivity, and overall well-being. Here are some effective stress management techniques:

1. Mindfulness and Meditation

- Practice Mindfulness: Spend a few minutes each day focusing on your breathing and staying present in the moment. This can help reduce anxiety and improve concentration.

- Meditation: Regular meditation can help calm your mind and reduce stress levels. Apps like Headspace or Calm can guide you through meditation practices.

2. Physical Activity

- Exercise Regularly: Engage in physical activities like walking, jogging, yoga, or any sport you enjoy. Exercise releases endorphins, which are natural stress relievers.

- Stretching: Incorporate stretching exercises into your daily routine to relieve tension and improve circulation.

3. Healthy Lifestyle

- Balanced Diet: Maintain a balanced diet with plenty of fruits, vegetables, and whole grains. Avoid excessive caffeine and sugar.

- Adequate Sleep: Ensure you get enough sleep every night. A well-rested mind is better equipped to handle stress.

4. Time Management

- Organize Your Schedule: Plan your study schedule in advance and stick to it. Breaking down your tasks into manageable chunks can reduce feelings of being overwhelmed.

- Prioritize Tasks: Focus on high-priority tasks first and avoid multitasking, which can increase stress levels.

5. Breaks and Leisure Activities

- Take Regular Breaks: Short breaks during study sessions can help refresh your mind. Use techniques like the Pomodoro Technique to schedule breaks.

- Leisure Activities: Engage in hobbies and activities you enjoy. Spending time doing what you love can be a great way to unwind.

6. Social Support

- Stay Connected: Keep in touch with family and friends. Sharing your feelings and experiences with loved ones can provide emotional support.

- Study Groups: Joining study groups can provide a sense of camaraderie and reduce the stress of studying alone.

7. Positive Thinking and Affirmations

- Positive Self-Talk: Replace negative thoughts with positive affirmations. Remind yourself of your strengths and achievements.

- Gratitude Journal: Keep a journal to write down things you are grateful for. Focusing on positive aspects of your life can improve your mood and reduce stress.

8. Professional Help

- Counseling: If stress becomes overwhelming, consider seeking help from a counselor or mental health professional.

- Workshops and Seminars: Attend stress management workshops or seminars to learn new techniques and strategies.

Example Relaxation Routine:

1. Morning: Start your day with a few minutes of mindfulness meditation.

2. Throughout the Day: Take short breaks every hour to stretch and breathe deeply.

3. Evening: Engage in a physical activity or hobby that you enjoy.

4. Before Bed: Write in your gratitude journal and practice a relaxation exercise, such as deep breathing or guided imagery.

Remember, managing stress is a continuous process. Incorporate these techniques into your daily routine to build resilience and maintain a positive mindset. You've got this! ?

BENEFITS OF YOGA AND MEDITATION

Yoga and meditation can be incredibly beneficial for CA students, helping to manage stress, improve focus, and enhance overall well-being. Here are some specific ways yoga and meditation can help, along with practical tips and exercises:

Benefits of Yoga and Meditation for CA Students

1. Reduces Stress and Anxiety:

- Both yoga and meditation help in calming the mind and reducing stress, which is especially important during the demanding CA exam preparation period.

2. Improves Focus and Concentration:

- Regular practice can enhance cognitive functions, leading to better concentration and memory retention.

3. Enhances Physical Health:

- Yoga improves flexibility, strength, and overall physical health, which can be beneficial when spending long hours studying.

4. Promotes Emotional Stability:

- Meditation helps in developing emotional resilience, allowing students to handle pressure and setbacks more effectively.

5. Boosts Energy Levels:

- Certain yoga poses and breathing techniques can boost energy levels, helping to combat fatigue and keep students alert.

Practical Yoga and Meditation Exercises

Yoga Poses:

1. Tadasana (Mountain Pose):

- Stand tall with feet together and arms by your side. Inhale deeply and stretch your arms upward, keeping your palms facing each other. Hold for a few breaths.

- Benefits: Improves posture, balance, and concentration.

2. Bhujangasana (Cobra Pose):

- Lie on your stomach with your hands under your shoulders. Inhale and lift your chest off the ground, keeping your elbows slightly bent. Hold for a few breaths.

- Benefits: Strengthens the spine, relieves stress, and boosts energy.

3. Balasana (Child's Pose):

- Kneel on the floor, sit back on your heels, and stretch your arms forward, lowering your forehead to the ground. Hold for a few breaths.

- Benefits: Relieves tension in the back, shoulders, and chest, promoting relaxation.

4. Vrikshasana (Tree Pose):

- Stand on one leg and place the sole of your other foot on your inner thigh or calf. Bring your palms together in front of your chest. Hold for a few breaths and switch legs.

- Benefits: Enhances balance and concentration.

<u>**Meditation Techniques:**</u>

1. Mindfulness Meditation:

- Sit comfortably and focus on your breath. Observe your thoughts without judgment, letting them pass like clouds. Practice for 10-15 minutes daily.

- Benefits: Increases awareness, reduces stress, and enhances emotional regulation.

2. Breath Awareness Meditation:

- Sit or lie down comfortably. Close your eyes and focus on your breath. Inhale deeply through your nose, hold for a few seconds, and exhale slowly through your mouth. Repeat for 5-10 minutes.

- Benefits: Calms the mind, reduces anxiety, and improves focus.

3. Guided Visualization:

- Close your eyes and imagine a peaceful place, such as a beach or forest. Visualize yourself there, engaging all your senses. Practice for 5-10 minutes.

- Benefits: Reduces stress and promotes relaxation.

Sample Daily Routine:

- Morning:

- Yoga Session: 15-20 minutes of yoga poses to energize your body and mind.

- Meditation: 10 minutes of mindfulness meditation to start the day with clarity.

- Midday:

- Short Break: Practice breath awareness meditation for 5 minutes to rejuvenate.

- Evening:

- Relaxation: 10 minutes of guided visualization to unwind and reduce stress before bed.

Incorporating yoga and meditation into your daily routine can significantly enhance your study efficiency, mental clarity, and overall well-being. Start with a few minutes each day and gradually increase the duration as you get more comfortable with the practices. Namaste! ??♂??

CHAPTER EIGHTY-SIX

BREATHING EXERCISES

Breathing exercises are a great way for CA students to reduce stress, improve concentration, and maintain overall well-being. Here are some simple yet effective breathing exercises that you can incorporate into your daily routine:

1. Diaphragmatic Breathing (Belly Breathing)

- How to Do It:

1. Sit or lie down in a comfortable position.

2. Place one hand on your chest and the other on your abdomen.

3. Inhale deeply through your nose, allowing your abdomen to rise while keeping your chest relatively still.

4. Exhale slowly through your mouth, letting your abdomen fall.

5. Repeat for 5-10 minutes.

2. 4-7-8 Breathing Technique

- How to Do It:

1. Sit comfortably with your back straight.

2. Inhale through your nose for a count of 4.

3. Hold your breath for a count of 7.

4. Exhale completely through your mouth for a count of 8.

5. Repeat for 4-8 cycles.

3. Box Breathing (Square Breathing)

- How to Do It:

1. Inhale through your nose for a count of 4.

2. Hold your breath for a count of 4.

3. Exhale through your mouth for a count of 4.

4. Hold your breath for a count of 4.

5. Repeat for 5-10 minutes.

4. Alternate Nostril Breathing (Nadi Shodhana)

- How to Do It:

1. Sit in a comfortable position with your spine straight.

2. Use your right thumb to close your right nostril.

3. Inhale deeply through your left nostril.

4. Close your left nostril with your right ring finger and release your right nostril.

5. Exhale through your right nostril.

6. Inhale through your right nostril, then close it with your right thumb.

7. Release your left nostril and exhale through your left nostril.

8. Repeat for 5-10 minutes.

5. Pursed Lip Breathing

- How to Do It:

1. Sit comfortably and relax your shoulders.

2. Inhale slowly through your nose for a count of 2.

3. Pucker your lips as if you're going to whistle.

4. Exhale slowly and gently through your pursed lips for a count of 4.

5. Repeat for 5-10 minutes.

Tips for Practicing Breathing Exercises:

- Consistency: Practice these exercises daily to build a habit and reap long-term benefits.

- Environment: Find a quiet, comfortable space where you can relax without distractions.

- Posture: Maintain good posture to allow for full lung expansion.

- Mindfulness: Focus on your breath and stay present in the moment, letting go of any distracting thoughts.

Incorporating these breathing exercises into your routine can help you stay calm, focused, and energized during your CA studies. Remember, a few minutes of mindful breathing can make a big difference in your overall well-being. ??

CHAPTER EIGHTY-SEVEN

RELAXING MUSIC FOR STRESS MANAGEMENT

Listening to relaxing music can be an excellent strategy for managing stress, especially for CA students. Here's how it can help and some tips for integrating it into your daily routine:

Benefits of Relaxing Music for Stress Management:

1. Reduces Anxiety: Gentle, soothing music can lower cortisol levels, the stress hormone, helping you feel more relaxed.

2. Improves Focus and Concentration: Background music can create a calm environment, making it easier to concentrate on your studies.

3. Enhances Mood: Uplifting music can boost your mood, making you feel more positive and motivated.

4. Promotes Better Sleep: Listening to calming music before bedtime can improve sleep quality, ensuring you wake up refreshed.

5. Lowers Heart Rate and Blood Pressure: Soft music can have a physiological effect, slowing your heart rate and lowering blood pressure.

CHAPTER EIGHTY-EIGHT

TIPS TO MAINTAIN HIGH ENERGY LEVELS

Maintaining high energy levels is crucial for CA students to stay focused and productive. Here are some practical tips to help keep your energy levels high:

Tips to Maintain High Energy Levels

1. Balanced Diet:

- Nutrient-Rich Foods: Incorporate a variety of fruits, vegetables, whole grains, lean proteins, and healthy fats into your diet.

- Frequent Small Meals: Eat small, balanced meals and snacks throughout the day to maintain steady blood sugar levels and prevent energy crashes.

- Stay Hydrated: Drink plenty of water throughout the day to stay hydrated. Dehydration can lead to fatigue.

2. Regular Exercise:

- Daily Activity: Engage in at least 30 minutes of physical activity daily, such as walking, jogging, or yoga, to boost your energy and mood.

- Stretching: Incorporate stretching exercises throughout the day to relieve muscle tension and improve circulation.

3. Adequate Sleep:

- Consistent Sleep Schedule: Maintain a regular sleep schedule by going to bed and waking up at the same time every day, even on weekends.

- Quality Sleep: Aim for 7-9 hours of quality sleep each night. Create a relaxing bedtime routine to improve sleep quality.

4. Effective Time Management:

- Study Breaks: Take regular breaks during study sessions to rest and recharge. Use techniques like the Pomodoro Technique to balance focused study periods with short breaks.

- Prioritize Tasks: Focus on high-priority tasks first to avoid unnecessary stress and fatigue.

5. Mindfulness and Relaxation:

- Meditation: Practice mindfulness or meditation to reduce stress and improve mental clarity. Even a few minutes of deep breathing can help.

- Relaxation Techniques: Incorporate relaxation techniques such as progressive muscle relaxation or guided imagery into your routine.

6. Stay Positive and Motivated:

- Set Goals: Set achievable study goals and reward yourself for meeting them. This can boost motivation and energy levels.

- Positive Mindset: Maintain a positive attitude and surround yourself with supportive people who encourage and motivate you.

By incorporating these habits into your daily routine, you can maintain high energy levels, enhance your focus, and improve your overall well-being. Stay consistent and listen to your body's needs to find what works best for you! ???

CHAPTER EIGHTY-NINE

EYE PROTECTION TIPS

Taking care of your eyes is crucial, especially when you're spending long hours studying for CA exams. Here are some tips for eye protection and exercises to reduce strain:

Eye Protection Tips

1. Use Computer Glasses: Consider using specialized computer glasses with anti-reflective coating and blue light filters to reduce glare and eye strain. Brands like Lenskart offer zero power glasses designed for screen use.

2. Adjust Screen Settings: Ensure your screen brightness is comfortable, and use a matte screen filter to reduce glare.

3. Maintain Proper Distance: Keep a distance of at least 20-28 inches from your screen.

4. Take Regular Breaks: Follow the 20-20-20 rule: Every 20 minutes, look at something 20 feet away for at least 20 seconds.

5. Proper Lighting: Ensure your study area is well-lit to reduce eye strain from poor lighting.

Eye Exercises

1. Eye Rolls: Slowly roll your eyes clockwise and then counter-clockwise.

2. Figure Eight: Trace a horizontal figure eight pattern with your eyes, then a vertical one.

3. Near-Far Focus Shifts: Hold a finger a few inches from your eyes and focus on it, then shift your focus to an object across the room.

4. Palming: Cup your hands over your closed eyes, creating slight pressure, and breathe deeply.

5. Blink Breaks: Blink rapidly for 10-15 seconds to refresh your eyes.

6. Zooming: Extend your arm with your thumb up, focus on your thumb, and bring it closer to your face, then extend it back out.

7. Diagonal Eye Stretches: Look diagonally up to the right, then down to the left, and vice versa.

8. Peripheral Awareness: Focus on an object in front of you and try to notice movements around you without moving your head.

9. Distance Gazing: Gaze at a distant object to give your eyes a break from close-up work.

Incorporating these practices into your daily routine can help reduce eye strain and keep your eyes healthy.

CHAPTER NINETY

SUCCESS IS NOT THE ABSENCE OF FAILURE

Handling failure effectively is a critical skill for CA students, given the challenging nature of the course. Here are some strategies to help you cope with and learn from setbacks:

Strategies for Handling Failure

1. Accept and Acknowledge:

- Recognition: Understand that failure is a part of the learning process. Accepting it allows you to move forward with a clearer perspective.

- Self-Compassion: Treat yourself with kindness and avoid harsh self-criticism. Everyone faces setbacks, and it's important to be gentle with yourself.

2. Analyze and Learn:

- Identify Mistakes: Reflect on what went wrong and identify the areas that need improvement. Understanding your mistakes is the first step toward avoiding them in the future.

- Seek Feedback: Discuss your performance with mentors, peers, or teachers to gain insights and suggestions for improvement.

3. Adjust Your Strategy:

- Revise Study Plan: Based on your analysis, revise your study plan. Focus more on weak areas and allocate time effectively.

- Practical Adjustments: Incorporate changes like better time management, improved study techniques, and regular revisions.

4. Stay Positive and Motivated:

- Positive Mindset: Maintain a positive attitude. Remind yourself of your goals and the progress you've made so far.

- Inspirational Stories: Read about successful individuals who faced setbacks but ultimately succeeded. Their stories can provide motivation and perspective.

5. Healthy Coping Mechanisms:

- Physical Activity: Engage in physical activities like exercise, yoga, or sports to reduce stress and improve your mood.

- Mindfulness Practices: Practice mindfulness or meditation to stay calm and focused. Techniques like deep breathing can help manage anxiety.

6. Support System:

- Connect with Peers: Talk to fellow CA students who may have faced similar challenges. Sharing experiences can provide comfort and support.

- Family and Friends: Lean on your family and friends for emotional support. They can provide encouragement and a listening ear.

7. Set Realistic Goals:

- Small Milestones: Set achievable short-term goals to build confidence and maintain motivation. Celebrate small victories along the way.

- Long-Term Vision: Keep your long-term goals in mind and use them as a driving force to overcome obstacles.

8. Professional Help:

- Counseling: If you're feeling overwhelmed, consider seeking help from a counselor or therapist. Professional support can provide strategies to cope with stress and setbacks.

Conclusion

Failure is not the end but a stepping stone towards success. By accepting and learning from it, adjusting your strategies, and maintaining a positive outlook, you can overcome setbacks and continue your journey towards becoming a Chartered Accountant.

Remember, resilience and perseverance are key traits of successful individuals. Keep pushing forward and believe in your ability to achieve your goals. You've got this! ???

CHAPTER NINETY-ONE

THOMAS EDISON: THE LIGHT BULB MOMENT

Thomas Edison, one of the greatest inventors of all time, is best known for inventing the electric light bulb. But his journey to success was filled with numerous failures.

Failures:

- Edison conducted over 10,000 unsuccessful experiments before finally creating a working light bulb. Each failure taught him what didn't work and brought him closer to finding a solution.

- He faced skepticism and criticism from his peers who doubted his ability to create a long-lasting light bulb.

Success:

- Instead of being discouraged, Edison famously said, "I have not failed. I've just found 10,000 ways that won't work."

- His perseverance paid off in 1879 when he finally succeeded in creating a practical and long-lasting electric light bulb, which revolutionized the world.

CHAPTER NINETY-TWO

ALEXANDER GRAHAM BELL: COMMUNICATING THROUGH FAILURE

Alexander Graham Bell, the inventor of the telephone, also faced numerous setbacks on his journey to success.

Failures:

- Bell conducted many failed experiments while trying to invent a device that could transmit sound electronically.

- His initial models and attempts were met with technical difficulties and failures.

Success:

- Bell's determination and innovative thinking led to the successful invention of the telephone in 1876.

- His invention changed the way people communicate and laid the foundation for modern telecommunications.

CHAPTER NINETY-THREE

NELSON MANDELA: TRIUMPH OVER ADVERSITY

Nelson Mandela, a global icon of peace and justice, faced immense challenges and failures throughout his life.

Failures:

- Mandela was imprisoned for 27 years for his fight against apartheid and racial discrimination in South Africa.

- During his imprisonment, he faced numerous personal and political setbacks.

Success:

- Despite the long years of imprisonment, Mandela never wavered in his commitment to justice and equality.

- After his release in 1990, he continued his efforts and became South Africa's first black president in 1994, leading the country towards reconciliation and equality.

These stories highlight the power of perseverance, determination, and the ability to learn from failures. They remind us that setbacks are an integral part of any journey to success and can be overcome with resilience and a positive mindset.

Stay inspired and keep pushing forward on your own journey!

CHAPTER NINETY-FOUR

THE COCKROACH THEORY BY SUNDAR PICHAI

The Cockroach Theory by Sundar Pichai is a powerful metaphor for handling life's challenges with composure and thoughtfulness. Here's a summary of the story and its lessons:

At a restaurant, a cockroach suddenly flew and landed on a lady. She panicked, screamed, and tried desperately to get rid of it. Her reaction caused a chain reaction, with everyone around her also panicking. The waiter, however, remained calm, observed the cockroach, and then calmly removed it.

The Lesson

Sundar Pichai used this story to illustrate that it's not the problem itself (the cockroach) that causes chaos, but our reaction to it. He emphasized the importance of responding thoughtfully rather than reacting instinctively. This approach can help manage stress, avoid unnecessary drama, and make better decisions.

Applying the Theory to CA Students

- Stay Calm: When faced with difficult exams or study challenges, stay composed and think clearly.

- Respond, Don't React: Take a moment to assess the situation before acting. Thoughtful responses lead to better outcomes.

- Focus on Solutions: Instead of getting overwhelmed by problems, focus on finding solutions.

By applying the Cockroach Theory, CA students can develop a more resilient and thoughtful approach to their studies and challenges.

CHAPTER NINETY-FIVE

DISTANCE YOURSELF FROM TOXIC PEOPLE

Navigating away from toxic people and finding a path to forgiveness can be challenging, especially for CA students who are already under significant pressure. Here are some steps that might help:

Steps to Distance Yourself from Toxic People:

1. Recognize Toxic Behavior: Understand and identify the signs of toxic behavior, such as constant negativity, manipulation, lack of respect, or undermining your efforts.
2. Set Boundaries: Firmly but politely establish boundaries. Make it clear what behavior you will not tolerate and stick to those boundaries.
3. Limit Interaction: Reduce the amount of time you spend with toxic individuals. Focus on surrounding yourself with supportive and positive people who encourage your growth.
4. Stay Focused on Your Goals: Keep your priorities and goals in mind. Let them guide your decisions and interactions, and don't let toxic behavior distract you from your path.
5. Seek Support: Talk to trusted friends, family members, or mentors who can offer advice and support. Sometimes, sharing your experiences with someone else can provide clarity and relief.

Steps to Forgive and Move On:

1. Acknowledge Your Feelings: It's important to recognize and validate your own emotions. Give yourself permission to feel hurt, anger, or disappointment.

2. Understand Their Perspective: Try to empathize with the person who hurt you. Understanding their motives or struggles doesn't excuse their behavior, but it can help you process your feelings.

3. Let Go of Resentment: Holding onto resentment can be draining. Focus on your own healing and well-being rather than the actions of others.

4. Focus on Personal Growth: Use the experience as a learning opportunity. Reflect on what you've gained from the situation and how it has made you stronger or more resilient.

5. Practice Self-Compassion: Be kind to yourself. Acknowledge your efforts to cope and move forward, and remember that forgiving someone is a process that takes time.

Practice Conversation:

You (Friend/Mentor): "It's not easy dealing with toxic people, especially when you're already under so much stress as a CA student. But remember, you have the power to set boundaries and protect your mental well-being. Surround yourself with those who uplift and support you. And when it comes to forgiveness, it's not about excusing their behavior but freeing yourself from the burden of negativity. Take it one step at a time, and focus on your own growth and healing."

Me (CA Student): "Thank you for the advice. I know it's important to set boundaries and not let toxic behavior affect me. I'll try to focus on my own goals and surround myself with positive influences. Forgiveness is tough, but I understand it's about letting go for my own peace of mind. I'll take it one day at a time."

CHAPTER NINETY-SIX

THE POWER OF FORGIVING

Forgiveness is often misunderstood as condoning or excusing someone's hurtful actions. However, true forgiveness is about liberating yourself from the burden of negative emotions like anger, resentment, and bitterness. It's a conscious decision to let go of the emotional hold that these feelings have over you, allowing you to find inner peace and move forward with your life. By choosing to forgive, you are not absolving the other person's behavior, but rather freeing yourself from the pain and turmoil it has caused. This act of releasing emotional baggage fosters personal growth, healing, and a sense of empowerment, enabling you to embrace a more positive and fulfilling future.

Here are some key reasons why forgiveness can be beneficial:

1. Emotional Freedom

- Release Negativity: Holding onto grudges or anger can weigh you down. Forgiveness allows you to release negative emotions and focus on positive ones.

- Reduce Stress: Letting go of resentment can reduce stress and anxiety, contributing to better mental health.

2. Improved Focus

- Clear Mind: Carrying emotional baggage can be distracting. By forgiving, you can clear your mind and concentrate better on your studies.

- Enhanced Productivity: Without the mental burden of unresolved conflicts, you can channel your energy more effectively into your academic pursuits.

3. Better Relationships

- Healthy Interactions: Forgiveness fosters healthier relationships, whether with peers, mentors, or family members. Positive relationships create a supportive environment for your studies.

- Empathy and Compassion: Learning to forgive can develop your empathy and compassion, making you more understanding and approachable.

4. Personal Growth

- Strength and Resilience: Forgiving toxic people can be a sign of inner strength and resilience. It shows that you are capable of rising above negativity.

- Self-Reflection: The process of forgiveness often involves self-reflection, helping you to understand your own emotions and reactions better.

Practical Steps to Forgiveness

1. Acknowledge Your Feelings: Recognize and accept your emotions. It's okay to feel hurt or angry.

2. Empathize: Try to understand the other person's perspective. This doesn't mean excusing their behavior, but it can help in letting go.

3. Express Yourself: If possible, communicate your feelings to the person involved. Use "I" statements to convey your emotions without blaming.

4. Set Boundaries: Forgiving doesn't mean allowing toxic behavior to continue. Set clear boundaries to protect your well-being.

5. Move Forward: Focus on the future and what you can control. Let go of the past and concentrate on your goals and aspirations.

Final Thoughts

Forgiveness is a powerful act that can free you from emotional burdens, allowing you to focus on what truly matters—your studies and personal growth. It's a journey that requires time and effort, but the benefits are well worth it. ?

CHAPTER NINETY-SEVEN

COMFORTABLE CLOTHING FOR CA STUDENTS

For CA students, comfort is key, especially during long study sessions and exams. Here are some clothing tips to keep you comfortable and focused:

1. Breathable Fabrics: Opt for cotton or moisture-wicking fabrics to stay cool and dry.

2. Loose-Fitting Clothes: Comfortable, loose-fitting shirts and trousers allow for better movement and airflow.

3. Layering: Wear layers so you can adjust to different temperatures easily.

4. Comfortable Footwear: Supportive shoes or sneakers that you can wear for extended periods.

5. Ergonomic Accessories: Consider ergonomic chairs and cushions to support your posture.

6. Minimal Accessories: Keep jewelry and accessories to a minimum to avoid distractions.

7. Personal Grooming: Ensure your hair is neatly styled and avoid heavy makeup that might feel uncomfortable.

These tips can help you stay comfortable and focused during your CA journey.

CHAPTER NINETY-EIGHT

EXAM DAY STRATEGIES

Exam day can be stressful, but with the right strategies, CA students can manage their nerves and perform at their best. Here are some effective exam day strategies:

Before the Exam

1. Preparation the Night Before:

- Review Key Points: Go through your summarized notes and key concepts. Avoid cramming new information.

- Set Out Materials: Prepare everything you need for the exam—admit card, pens, calculator, water bottle, etc.

- Sleep Well: Ensure you get a good night's sleep. Aim for at least 7-8 hours to be well-rested.

2. Morning Routine:

- Healthy Breakfast: Have a nutritious breakfast that includes complex carbohydrates and proteins to sustain your energy levels.

- Stay Hydrated: Drink plenty of water to stay hydrated but avoid excessive caffeine.

- Relaxation Techniques: Practice deep breathing or meditation to calm your nerves.

3. Positive Mindset:

- Affirmations: Use positive affirmations to boost your confidence, such as "I am well-prepared and capable."

- Visualize Success: Imagine yourself completing the exam successfully and feeling accomplished.

During the Exam

1. Arrive Early:

- Reach the exam center early to avoid last-minute stress and settle into the environment.

2. Read Instructions Carefully:

- Spend a few minutes reading the instructions thoroughly before starting the exam. Make sure you understand the format and marking scheme.

3. Manage Your Time:

- Allocate time to each section based on the marks assigned. Keep an eye on the clock to ensure you can complete all sections.

- Answer Easy Questions First: Start with questions you are confident about to build momentum and gain confidence.

- Flag Difficult Questions: Mark questions that are challenging and come back to them later.

4. Stay Calm and Focused:

- If you feel anxious, take deep breaths to calm yourself.

- Focus on one question at a time. Avoid worrying about the entire paper.

5. Review Your Answers:

- If time permits, review your answers before submitting. Check for any mistakes or omissions.

6. Avoid Negative Thoughts:

- Don't dwell on questions you found difficult. Focus on the next task and keep a positive attitude throughout the exam.

After the Exam

1. Relax and Unwind:

- Take some time to relax and unwind after the exam. Engage in activities you enjoy to de-stress.

2. Reflect on Your Performance:

- Reflect on what went well and identify areas for improvement for future exams.

3. Move On to the Next Goal:

- Don't dwell too much on the exam that just passed. Start preparing for the next subject or task.

By following these strategies, you can approach your CA exams with confidence and poise. Remember, your preparation and hard work will pay off. Best of luck! ?

CHAPTER NINETY-NINE

POST-EXAM STRATEGIES

Once you've completed your CA exams, it's important to plan your next steps effectively to ensure continued growth and success. Here are some strategies for CA students to plan for the next level:

1. Evaluate Your Exam Performance

- Reflect and Assess: Review your performance in the exams. Identify strengths and areas that need improvement.

- Feedback: Seek feedback from mentors or peers to gain insights on how to improve further.

2. Set New Goals

- Short-Term Goals: Set specific, achievable short-term goals such as gaining practical experience, learning new skills, or starting the next level of studies.

- Long-Term Goals: Define your long-term career goals, such as becoming a partner in a firm, starting your own practice, or specializing in a particular area of accounting.

3. Plan Further Studies or Certifications

- Advanced Courses: Consider enrolling in advanced courses or certifications related to your field. This could include courses on taxation, auditing, or financial management.

- Professional Development: Stay updated with the latest industry trends and regulations by attending workshops, seminars, and conferences.

4. Gain Practical Experience

- Internships and Training: Seek internships or training opportunities to gain hands-on experience. Practical exposure is invaluable in applying theoretical knowledge.

- Networking: Connect with professionals in your field through networking events, alumni associations, or online platforms like LinkedIn.

5. Build a Strong Resume

- Update Your CV: Add your latest achievements, skills, and experiences to your resume.

- Cover Letter: Prepare a compelling cover letter that highlights your strengths and career aspirations.

6. Job Search Strategies

- Research Potential Employers: Identify companies or firms that align with your career goals.

- Apply Strategically: Tailor your applications to each job, showcasing how your skills and experiences make you a good fit for the role.

7. Continuous Learning and Skill Development

- Soft Skills: Develop essential soft skills like communication, leadership, and time management.

- Technical Skills: Enhance your technical skills by learning new software or tools commonly used in the industry.

8. Stay Motivated and Positive

- Celebrate Achievements: Take time to celebrate your accomplishments, no matter how small.

- Stay Positive: Maintain a positive mindset and be open to learning from both successes and setbacks.

By setting clear goals, seeking continuous improvement, and staying proactive, you can successfully transition to the next level of your career journey as a CA professional. You've already accomplished so much, and the future holds even more opportunities for growth and success! ?

CAREER OPPORTUNITIES FOR CHARTERED ACCOUNTANTS

A Chartered Accountant (CA) qualification opens a vast array of career opportunities across different sectors. Here are some prominent career paths for CA professionals:

1. Auditing and Assurance:

- Internal Auditor: Ensure that the company's internal controls, risk management processes, and governance are effective and efficient.

- External Auditor: Perform independent examinations of financial statements to provide an opinion on their accuracy and compliance with regulations.

2. Financial Accounting and Reporting:

- Financial Analyst: Analyze financial data, create reports, and provide insights to aid decision-making.

- Financial Controller: Oversee the preparation of financial statements, budgeting, and financial reporting processes.

3. Taxation:

- Tax Consultant: Provide advice on tax planning, compliance, and strategies to optimize tax liabilities.

- Indirect Tax Specialist: Focus on GST, VAT, customs duties, and other indirect taxes.

4. Consulting:

- Management Consultant: Advise organizations on improving performance, solving problems, and implementing effective strategies.

- Risk Consultant: Identify, assess, and mitigate financial and operational risks.

5. Corporate Finance:

- Investment Banker: Assist companies in raising capital, mergers and acquisitions, and other financial transactions.

- Corporate Treasurer: Manage the organization's financial assets, liabilities, and investment strategies.

6. Forensic Accounting:

- Forensic Accountant: Investigate financial discrepancies, fraud, and litigation support.

- Fraud Examiner: Detect, investigate, and prevent financial fraud.

7. Information Technology:

- IT Auditor: Assess the effectiveness of an organization's information systems and internal controls.

- Systems Analyst: Design and implement IT systems to improve business processes.

8. Public Sector:

- Government Accountant: Work in various government departments to manage public funds and ensure compliance with financial regulations.

- Regulatory Compliance Officer: Ensure organizations comply with laws and regulations, especially in financial and corporate governance.

9. Education and Research:

- Academic Lecturer: Teach accounting and finance subjects at universities and educational institutions.

- Research Analyst: Conduct research on financial, economic, and accounting trends and issues.

10. Entrepreneurship:

- Startup Founder: Use your financial acumen to start and grow your own business.

- Business Advisor: Provide consultancy services to small and medium enterprises (SMEs).

11. Financial Services:

- Portfolio Manager: Manage investment portfolios for individuals or institutions.

- Credit Analyst: Assess the creditworthiness of organizations and individuals applying for loans.

Specialized Fields:

- International Accounting: Work with multinational companies and handle cross-border financial issues.

- Environmental Accounting: Focus on sustainability and environmental impact reporting.

- Insurance: Manage financial aspects of insurance companies, including risk assessment and policy pricing.

Non-Traditional Roles:

- Content Creation: Develop educational content and materials for accounting students and professionals.

- Financial Journalism: Write and report on financial news, trends, and insights.

Additional Certifications:

- Chartered Financial Analyst (CFA): Specialize in investment management.

- Certified Public Accountant (CPA): Gain global recognition and expand career opportunities internationally.

A CA qualification equips you with a versatile skill set that can be applied in numerous roles and industries. Whether you choose to work in a traditional accounting role or explore non-traditional paths, the opportunities are vast and rewarding. ?

NETWORKING AND PROFESSIONAL DEVELOPMENT

Post-qualification, networking and professional development become even more crucial for Chartered Accountants (CAs) to advance their careers and stay relevant in the dynamic field of finance and accounting. Here are some strategies to help you grow and thrive in your career:

Networking Strategies for Qualified CAs

1. Professional Associations

- Join Professional Bodies: Continue your involvement with professional bodies like the Institute of Chartered Accountants of India (ICAI) or similar organizations. Attend their events, workshops, and seminars.

- Special Interest Groups: Join special interest groups within these associations that focus on your areas of interest, such as taxation, auditing, or corporate finance.

2. Industry Conferences and Events

- Attend Conferences: Participate in industry conferences, both national and international. These events provide opportunities to network with peers, learn about industry trends, and meet potential employers or clients.

- Speak at Events: If possible, present papers or speak at these events. This not only enhances your profile but also establishes you as a thought leader in your field.

3. Mentorship Programs

- Find a Mentor: Seek out experienced professionals who can guide you in your career. A mentor can offer valuable advice, support, and networking opportunities.

- Be a Mentor: Mentoring junior professionals can also expand your network and establish you as a leader in your field.

4. Social Media and Online Presence

- LinkedIn: Keep your LinkedIn profile updated with your latest achievements, skills, and experiences. Join relevant groups and participate in discussions.

- Professional Blogs: Start a blog or contribute to industry publications. Sharing your insights and experiences can help you connect with a broader audience.

5. Networking Events

- Host or Attend Networking Events: Attend networking events organized by firms, professional bodies, or alumni associations. Hosting your own events can also be a great way to build your network.

Professional Development Strategies for Qualified CAs

1. Continuing Professional Education (CPE)

- Mandatory CPE Credits: Ensure you meet the mandatory CPE requirements set by your professional body. Attend courses, seminars, and webinars to earn these credits.

- Advanced Certifications: Pursue advanced certifications in areas like IFRS, forensic accounting, or financial planning to deepen your expertise.

2. Specialization

- Identify a Niche: Specialize in a particular area of interest, such as tax advisory, financial consulting, or forensic accounting. Specialization can set you apart in the job market.

- Advanced Degrees: Consider pursuing an MBA or a related master's degree to further your knowledge and career prospects.

3. Skill Enhancement

- Soft Skills: Continuously work on your communication, leadership, and interpersonal skills. These are crucial for career advancement.

- Technical Skills: Stay updated with the latest accounting software, data analytics tools, and technologies relevant to your field.

4. Stay Updated with Industry Trends

- Read Industry Publications: Subscribe to industry journals, magazines, and newsletters to stay informed about the latest trends and developments.

- Professional Forums: Join online forums and discussion groups where industry professionals share insights and experiences.

5. Practical Experience

- Project Involvement: Take on diverse projects that challenge you and expand your expertise. Practical experience is invaluable for professional growth.

- Cross-Functional Teams: Work in cross-functional teams to gain a broader perspective and enhance your collaborative skills.

By actively engaging in networking and professional development, you can build a strong foundation for a successful career as a Chartered Accountant. These efforts will not only enhance your knowledge and skills but also open doors to new opportunities and connections.

CONTINUING EDUCATION AND SPECIALIZATIONS

Continuing education and specialization are critical for Chartered Accountants (CAs) to stay competitive and advance in their careers. Here are some options and strategies for post-qualification education and specialization:

Continuing Education

1. Advanced Degrees

- MBA (Master of Business Administration): Pursuing an MBA can provide a broader understanding of business management and open up leadership roles.

- Master's in Finance or Accounting: These programs offer in-depth knowledge and can enhance your expertise in specific areas like financial analysis, auditing, or taxation.

2. Professional Certifications

- CFA (Chartered Financial Analyst): Ideal for those interested in investment management, financial analysis, and portfolio management.

- CMA (Certified Management Accountant): Focuses on strategic management and financial management, beneficial for roles in corporate finance and management accounting.

- CPA (Certified Public Accountant): If you plan to work internationally, especially in the USA, this certification is highly regarded.

3. Specialized Courses

- IFRS (International Financial Reporting Standards): Understanding IFRS is crucial for working in multinational corporations or in countries that follow these standards.

- Forensic Accounting and Fraud Detection: Courses in forensic accounting can prepare you for roles in fraud examination and forensic investigations.

- Risk Management: Specializing in risk management can be valuable for roles in internal audit, compliance, and financial risk assessment.

4. Continuous Professional Education (CPE)

- ICAI Programs: Participate in ICAI's CPE programs to stay updated with the latest developments in accounting standards, regulations, and best practices.

- Workshops and Seminars: Attend industry workshops and seminars to gain practical insights and network with professionals.

Specialization Options

1. Taxation

- Direct Taxation: Specialize in income tax, corporate tax, and international taxation.

- Indirect Taxation: Focus on GST, customs, and other indirect taxes.

2. Audit and Assurance

- Statutory Audit: Gain expertise in statutory audits for companies and organizations.

- Internal Audit: Specialize in internal control assessments, risk management, and compliance audits.

3. Financial Management

- Corporate Finance: Specialize in financial planning, capital budgeting, and corporate restructuring.

- Investment Banking: Focus on mergers and acquisitions, IPOs, and financial advisory services.

4. Forensic Accounting

- Fraud Examination: Become an expert in detecting and preventing financial fraud.

- Litigation Support: Provide expert testimony and support in legal cases involving financial disputes.

5. Consulting

- Management Consulting: Provide strategic advice to businesses on improving performance and solving complex problems.

- IT Consulting: Focus on the integration of IT systems and financial processes.

Steps to Pursue Specialization

1. Identify Your Interest: Reflect on your career goals and interests to choose a specialization that aligns with your aspirations.

2. Research Programs: Look for reputable institutions and programs that offer the specialization you are interested in.

3. Enroll in Courses: Register for courses and certifications that will equip you with the necessary knowledge and skills.

4. Gain Practical Experience: Seek opportunities to apply your learning through internships, projects, or part-time roles in your chosen specialization.

5. Network with Experts: Connect with professionals in your field to gain insights and guidance on building a successful career in your specialization.

Conclusion

Continuing education and specialization are essential for advancing your career as a Chartered Accountant. By staying updated with industry trends and gaining expertise in specific areas, you can enhance your professional value and open up new opportunities for growth.

INSPIRATIONAL STORIES SUCCESS STORIES OF CA STUDENTS ON THEIR JOURNEY

1. The Determined Dreamer: Priya's Journey

Priya always dreamt of becoming a Chartered Accountant despite coming from a non-commerce background. She faced numerous challenges, including financial constraints. However, her determination never wavered. Priya devised a rigorous study schedule, utilized free online resources, and sought mentorship from practicing CAs. Her hard work paid off, and she cleared her CA exams on the first attempt, proving that with dedication and smart work, any dream can be achieved.

2. The Second Chance: Raj's Revival

Raj attempted the CA exams twice and faced failure each time. He was disheartened but decided to give it one more try. This time, he changed his approach. He focused on understanding concepts rather than rote learning and joined a study group for better support. Raj also practiced mindfulness to manage stress. His perseverance and strategic changes led him to clear all exams in his third attempt, showing that failure is not the end but a step towards success.

3. The Late Bloomer: Meera's Success

Meera started her CA journey later in life after having a family. Balancing family responsibilities and studies was tough, but she was determined. Meera created a flexible study schedule, involving her family in her plans, and used every free moment for revision. Meera's story is a testament to the fact that it's never too late to pursue your dreams.

4. The Overcomer: Amit's Story

Amit struggled with a learning disability that made traditional studying methods challenging. Instead of giving up, he sought alternative ways to learn, like visual aids and interactive learning platforms. Amit also worked closely with his tutors to tailor his study approach. His determination and innovative methods led him to clear his CA exams, proving that with the right support and strategies, obstacles can be overcome.

5. The Fighter: Neha's Battle

Neha was diagnosed with a serious illness during her CA preparation. She had to undergo treatment while studying, which drained her physically and emotionally. Despite this, she never gave up. Neha studied whenever she felt a little better and stayed connected with her study group for moral support. Her resilience and fighting spirit saw her through, and she passed her exams, showing that true strength lies in never giving up.

6. The Innovator: Rahul's Approach

Rahul realized that traditional study methods weren't working for him. He started creating his own study materials, including flashcards and mind maps. He also formed a peer group where they taught each other different subjects. This innovative approach not only helped Rahul understand the material better but also improved his retention. He cleared his exams with flying colours, illustrating that sometimes thinking outside the box is the key to success.

7. The Visionary: Karan's Goal

Karan always visualized himself as a successful CA. He made vision boards, wrote down his goals, and regularly visualized his success. This positive reinforcement kept him motivated and focused. Karan's story shows that a clear vision and positive mindset can propel you towards your goals.

8. The Networker: Sita's Support

Sita understood the power of networking early in her CA journey. She attended seminars, joined online forums, and connected with fellow CA aspirants and professionals. This network provided her with valuable resources, guidance, and moral support. Sita cleared her exams successfully, underlining the importance of a strong support system and community.

9. The Self-Motivated: Arjun's Drive

Arjun didn't have access to coaching classes due to financial constraints. However, his self-motivation and disciplined approach led him to success. He used free resources available online, created a strict study regimen, and stayed committed to his goal. Arjun's story is a powerful reminder that self-motivation and discipline can lead to great achievements.

These stories demonstrate that with determination, innovative strategies, and the right support, any CA student can overcome challenges and achieve their goals. Keep believing in yourself, stay motivated, and never give up on your dreams. You've got this! ???

The story of the butterfly and the cocoon

The story of the butterfly and the cocoon is a powerful metaphor for growth and resilience, perfect for CA students.

The Story

A man found a cocoon and decided to watch the butterfly emerge. One day, a small opening appeared. The man watched as the butterfly struggled to force its body through the tiny hole. It seemed to stop making progress, appearing stuck. The man, out of kindness, decided to help. He gently snipped the cocoon to widen the hole. The butterfly emerged easily, but its body was swollen, and its wings were shriveled. The man expected the wings to expand and the butterfly to fly, but it never did. The butterfly spent its life crawling with weak wings.

The man didn't realize that the struggle to emerge from the cocoon was nature's way of forcing fluid from the butterfly's body into its wings, making it ready for flight. Without the struggle, the butterfly was crippled.

Lessons for CA Students

1. Embrace Challenges:

- Growth Through Struggle: Like the butterfly, CA students need to embrace the challenges and struggles of their studies. These difficulties are essential for growth and preparation.

2. Self-Reliance:

- Independence: Just as the butterfly needed to rely on its own efforts, CA students must develop self-reliance and problem-solving skills to succeed.

3. Patience:

- Trust the Process: Understand that true growth and success take time and effort. Be patient with yourself and trust the process of learning.

4. Resilience:

- Strength Through Adversity: Challenges and setbacks are opportunities to build resilience. Every difficult topic or exam is a chance to become stronger and more prepared.

Applying the Story to CA Studies

1. Face Difficult Topics: Don't shy away from tough subjects. The effort you put into understanding them will make you stronger and more knowledgeable.

2. Practice Patience: Trust that your consistent efforts will pay off in the long run. Growth takes time.

3. Build Resilience: Use setbacks as learning opportunities. Analyze what went wrong and how you can improve.

4. Develop Self-Reliance: Strengthen your problem-solving skills. While collaboration is important, being able to rely on yourself is crucial.

Just like the butterfly needs to struggle to become strong, CA students must embrace the challenges of their journey. These struggles prepare you for the exams and for a successful career ahead.

The story of the Tortoise and the Hare.

The story of the Tortoise and the Hare is a classic fable that holds valuable lessons for CA students. Here are four versions of the story, each with a unique twist:

Version 1: The Classic Tale

The Race Begins

The hare and the tortoise agree to a race. The hare, confident in his speed, dashes ahead and soon leaves the tortoise far behind. Believing he has plenty of time, the hare decides to take a nap. Meanwhile, the slow and steady tortoise keeps moving forward. Eventually, the tortoise overtakes the sleeping hare and wins the race.

Lesson: Slow and steady wins the race. Consistency and perseverance are key to success.

Version 2: The Hare Learns His Lesson

The Rematch

After losing the first race, the hare realizes his mistake. He challenges the tortoise to another race but this time, he doesn't stop to rest. Both the hare and the tortoise maintain their pace, but the hare's speed ensures his victory.

Lesson: Talent and effort combined with consistency lead to success.

Version 3: The Collaborative Approach

Teamwork Wins

The tortoise and the hare decide to race again but this time, they choose to run as a team. The hare carries the tortoise on his back for the flat portions of the race, while the tortoise carries the hare through the rough, rocky terrains. Together, they reach the finish line in record time.

Lesson: Teamwork and leveraging each other's strengths can achieve greater success.

Version 4: Innovation and Adaptability

The Modern Race

In a modern twist, the race involves multiple terrains—water, mountains, and plains. The tortoise, being versatile, easily crosses the water section, climbs steadily over mountains, and walks briskly on plains. The hare, though fast, struggles with the water and mountains. The tortoise's adaptability and strategic use of different tools help him win the race.

Lesson: Adaptability and strategic thinking are crucial for overcoming diverse challenges.

Applying the Lessons to CA Studies

- Classic Tale: Consistent study habits and perseverance are essential.

- Hare's Rematch: Combine your innate talents with consistent effort.

- Teamwork: Collaborate with peers and leverage each other's strengths.

- Adaptability: Be flexible and use various study tools and methods to excel.

The story of tree roots slowly breaking a rock

The story of tree roots slowly breaking a rock is a powerful metaphor for persistence and steady progress, especially for CA students. Here's how the story goes and its lessons for you:

The Story

Once upon a time, there was a rock, solid and seemingly impenetrable. Nearby, a small tree began to grow. The tree's roots were tiny and fragile compared to the rock's solid mass. However, over time, the roots began to find small cracks and crevices in the rock.

Slowly but persistently, the roots worked their way into these tiny openings. Day by day, they exerted gentle pressure. It seemed impossible that these delicate roots could affect the sturdy rock, but they continued their patient work without giving up.

Years passed, and the relentless pressure of the roots began to make a difference. The rock started to crack and, eventually, split apart, allowing the tree to grow even stronger and taller, flourishing in the space it had created.

Lessons for CA Students

1. Persistence Pays Off:

- Just like the roots, steady and continuous effort in your studies will eventually lead to success. Don't be disheartened by slow progress.

2. Small Steps Matter:

- The roots didn't break the rock in a single attempt. They made progress bit by bit. Similarly, small, consistent study sessions can lead to significant improvement over time.

3. Utilize Opportunities:

- The roots found tiny cracks to make their way in. Look for small opportunities to learn and grow, whether it's a few extra minutes of study or a practice question.

4. Overcoming Challenges:

- The rock seemed unbreakable, but persistent effort overcame it. Face your toughest subjects and challenges head-on with determination.

Applying the Lessons to CA Studies

1. Consistent Study Routine: Establish a regular study schedule and stick to it. Even short, daily study sessions add up.

2. Patience and Perseverance: Understand that mastery takes time. Be patient with your progress and keep pushing forward.

3. Seize Small Opportunities: Utilize even small pockets of time for quick reviews or practice problems.

4. Stay Determined: Believe in your ability to overcome difficult subjects and keep working towards your goals.

By embodying the patience and persistence of tree roots, CA students can steadily and surely achieve their goals, no matter how challenging the journey might seem. Remember, your continuous efforts will eventually crack open even the hardest challenges, just like the roots breaking the rock.

The Tale of the Wheel and Its Lesson

In a time when the world was young and humans were just beginning to harness the power of nature, there lived a brilliant inventor named Elara. She resided in a village surrounded by vast plains and rolling hills. The villagers admired her ingenuity, for Elara had a knack for creating tools that made life easier and more productive.

Elara's Invention

One day, while observing a group of villagers struggling to transport heavy loads of grain, Elara had an idea. She noticed that rolling objects were much easier to move than dragging them. Inspired, she went to her workshop and began experimenting. After several attempts, she crafted a circular object made of wood and attached it to a sturdy axle. Elara had invented the wheel.

The Transformation

Elara demonstrated her invention to the villagers. With the wheel, they could easily transport heavy loads with minimal effort. The villagers were amazed and grateful, and soon, wheels were used for carts, wagons, and other purposes. The invention of the wheel transformed their daily lives, making tasks more efficient and less laborious.

The Unwillingness to Adapt

Years passed, and Elara's village flourished. However, in a nearby village, the people continued to struggle with manual labor. They had heard of Elara's wheel but were reluctant to adopt it, believing their traditional methods were sufficient. Their stubbornness resulted in slower progress and greater physical strain.

The King's Wisdom

One day, the king visited the nearby village and witnessed their struggles. He called the village elders and shared a lesson: "Invention is a gift that can propel us forward. There is no need to reinvent the wheel when it already exists. Embrace the tools and knowledge available to you, for they can lead to greater efficiency and success."

The village elders took the king's words to heart and decided to adopt the wheel. They quickly realized the benefits and soon caught up with Elara's village in terms of productivity and prosperity.

The Lesson for CA Students

For CA students, the tale of the wheel teaches a valuable lesson: There is no need to reinvent the wheel when preparing for exams and pursuing your goals. Using established tools and techniques can significantly enhance your learning and performance.

The Story of the Thirsty Crow

The story of the Thirsty Crow is a classic fable that offers valuable lessons in problem-solving, resourcefulness, and persistence, which are highly relevant for CA students. Here's how the story goes and its lessons for your studies:

The Story of the Thirsty Crow

On a hot summer day, a thirsty crow flew over the fields searching for water. For a long time, he could not find any. Feeling weak and exhausted, he suddenly spotted a pitcher with a little water at the bottom.

The crow tried to drink the water, but his beak couldn't reach it. He thought hard and noticed some pebbles nearby. He picked up the pebbles one by one and dropped them into the pitcher. As more and more pebbles filled the pitcher, the water level rose higher and higher. Eventually, it was high enough for the crow to drink. The crow quenched his thirst and flew away, satisfied and refreshed.

Lessons for CA Students

1. Creative Problem-Solving

- The crow faced a seemingly insurmountable problem but found a creative solution by using pebbles to raise the water level. CA students should think outside the box and find innovative ways to tackle difficult study topics.

2. Persistence and Patience

- The crow didn't give up when the task seemed impossible. He patiently picked up one pebble at a time. Similarly, CA students need to be persistent and patient, breaking down large tasks into manageable steps.

The story of the Thirsty Crow is a classic fable that offers valuable lessons in problem-solving, resourcefulness, and persistence, which are highly relevant for CA students. Here's how the story goes and its lessons for your studies:

The Story of the Thirsty Crow

On a hot summer day, a thirsty crow flew over the fields searching for water. For a long time, he could not find any. Feeling weak and exhausted, he suddenly spotted a pitcher with a little water at the bottom.

The crow tried to drink the water, but his beak couldn't reach it. He thought hard and noticed some pebbles nearby. He picked up the pebbles one by one and dropped them into the pitcher. As more and more pebbles filled the pitcher, the water level rose higher and higher. Eventually, it was high enough for the crow to drink. The crow quenched his thirst and flew away, satisfied and refreshed.

Lessons for CA Students

1. Creative Problem-Solving

- The crow faced a seemingly insurmountable problem but found a creative solution by using pebbles to raise the water level. CA students should think outside the box and find innovative ways to tackle difficult study topics.

2. Persistence and Patience

- The crow didn't give up when the task seemed impossible. He patiently picked up one pebble at a time. Similarly, CA students need to be persistent and patient, breaking down large tasks into manageable steps.

3. Resourcefulness

- The crow used the resources available to him to solve the problem. CA students should make the best use of their study materials, resources, and support systems to succeed.

4. Step-by-Step Approach

- The crow's method of dropping pebbles one by one highlights the importance of a step-by-step approach. Focus on small, consistent efforts to achieve your larger goals.

Applying the Lessons to Your CA Journey

1. Creative Study Techniques: Use creative methods like mnemonics, visual aids, and mind maps to understand and remember complex concepts.

2. Break Down Tasks: Divide your study material into smaller sections and tackle them one at a time. Consistent effort will lead to progress.

3. Use Available Resources: Utilize all available resources, such as textbooks, online courses, study groups, and mentors.

4. Stay Persistent: Keep a positive attitude and remain persistent, even when the journey gets tough. Small, consistent actions will lead to success.

By adopting the lessons from the story of the Thirsty Crow, CA students can develop problem-solving skills, patience, and resourcefulness, leading to a successful and rewarding journey.

The Story of Sharpening the Axe

Once upon a time, two woodcutters, Ram and Shyam, decided to compete to see who could cut down more trees in a day. Both were equally skilled and used similar axes.

At dawn, they began their task. Ram started chopping away at trees immediately, with great determination. He worked tirelessly, not stopping even for a break. Shyam, on the other hand, took regular breaks throughout the day. Ram felt confident that he would win since Shyam seemed to be wasting time.

However, as the sun set and the competition ended, it turned out that Shyam had cut down significantly more trees than Ram. Ram was astonished and asked Shyam how he had managed to outperform him despite taking so many breaks.

Shyam smiled and replied, "What you didn't see during my breaks was that I was sharpening my axe. A sharp axe cuts more efficiently than a blunt one."

Lessons for CA Students

1. Preparation and Skill Enhancement

- Sharpening the Axe: Just as Shyam took time to sharpen his axe, CA students should invest time in sharpening their skills and enhancing their knowledge.

- Action: Regularly review and update your study materials. Practice problem-solving and keep improving your understanding of key concepts.

2. Work Smarter, Not Just Harder

- Efficiency Over Effort: Ram worked hard without breaks, while Shyam worked smarter by maintaining his tool. Similarly, effective study techniques can yield better results than simply putting in long hours.

- Action: Use effective study techniques like the Pomodoro Technique, mind mapping, and active learning to make your study sessions more productive.

3. Importance of Rest and Breaks

- Regular Breaks: Shyam's breaks were not just for rest but to ensure his tool was in top condition. CA students should take regular breaks to rest and rejuvenate their minds.

- Action: Incorporate short breaks into your study schedule to avoid burnout and maintain mental sharpness.

4. Continuous Improvement

- Ongoing Learning: Sharpening the axe symbolizes continuous improvement. CA students should strive for continuous learning and self-improvement.

- Action: Attend workshops, join study groups, and seek feedback to keep refining your skills and knowledge.

Practical Application for CA Students

1. Daily Review Sessions: Dedicate time each day to review and revise previously learned material.

2. Practice Exams: Regularly take mock tests and practice exams to assess your understanding and identify areas for improvement.

3. Study Techniques: Use a variety of study techniques to keep your sessions engaging and effective.

4. Healthy Routine: Maintain a balanced lifestyle with proper sleep, nutrition, and exercise to keep your mind and body in optimal condition.

5. Seek Guidance: Don't hesitate to seek help from mentors, teachers, or peers when needed. Collaboration can provide new insights and

perspectives.

By embracing the lessons from the story of sharpening the axe, CA students can enhance their study efficiency, continuously improve their skills, and achieve greater success in their exams.

Ready to sharpen your axe and study more effectively?

GEARING UP FOR GREATNESS: BUILDING FORWARD MOMENTUM

Building momentum is like starting a car and moving forward with purpose. Just as a car needs ignition and steady acceleration to gain speed, achieving your goals requires initial effort and sustained progress. The key is to kickstart your journey with determination and keep pushing through challenges. As you gather momentum, each step forward becomes easier and more rewarding, driving you closer to your dreams. The engine of progress roars to life when fueled by persistence and a clear vision, propelling you towards success with unstoppable force. Embrace the journey, accelerate with confidence, and watch as your momentum carries you to new heights.

Building forward momentum in your studies is crucial, much like getting a car to start and move efficiently. Here's an analogy to illustrate this process for CA students:

Starting the Car

1. Ignition (Initiating Study)

- Analogy: When you turn the key in the ignition, you're initiating the car's engine. Similarly, starting your study session requires an initial push. This could be setting a specific time to start studying each day.

- Action: Schedule a consistent start time for your study sessions. This routine acts as your ignition, helping you get started without procrastination.

Building Speed

2. First Gear (Initial Progress)

- Analogy: In first gear, the car moves slowly but steadily. This initial phase might feel slow as you get into the rhythm.

- Action: Begin with easier or more interesting subjects to build confidence and make the initial progress less daunting. This can help you ease into your study flow.

3. Shifting Gears (Increasing Efficiency)

- Analogy: As the car gains speed, you shift to higher gears for better efficiency. Once you're comfortable, you can tackle more challenging subjects.

- Action: Gradually increase the complexity of the topics you study.

Maintaining Momentum

4. Cruising Speed (Steady Study Routine)

- Analogy: At cruising speed, the car moves smoothly and efficiently. Maintaining a steady pace helps you cover more distance without burnout.

- Action: Establish a steady study routine. Consistency is key. Stick to your schedule and make studying a daily habit to maintain momentum.

Dealing with Obstacles

5. Roadblocks and Traffic (Overcoming Challenges)

- Analogy: Just like a car encounters traffic or roadblocks, you might face distractions or difficult topics.

- Action: Identify and minimize distractions. When facing tough topics, break them down into smaller parts or seek help from peers or mentors.

Refueling

6. Fuel and Maintenance (Self-Care)

- Analogy: Cars need fuel and regular maintenance to keep running smoothly. Similarly, you need to take care of your physical and mental well-being.

- Action: Ensure you get enough sleep, eat a balanced diet, and take breaks to recharge. Regular exercise and mindfulness practices can also help maintain your overall health.

Example Study Plan Using the Car Analogy

1. Ignition: Start studying at 9 AM every day.

2. First Gear: Begin with an easy subject or revision of previously learned material.

3. Shifting Gears: After 30 minutes, move on to a more challenging topic.

4. Cruising Speed: Study for 2 hours with short breaks

5. Roadblocks: If you encounter a difficult topic, break it down, and tackle it in smaller chunks.

6. Refueling: Take a 20-minute break after every 2-hour study session. Use this time for a healthy snack, a short walk, or relaxation exercises.

By using this car analogy, CA students can understand how to build and maintain study momentum effectively, ensuring a smooth and productive journey towards their academic goals.

POWER LIES IN THE APPLICATION OF KNOWLEDGE, NOT JUST ITS POSSESSION.

In the journey of becoming a Chartered Accountant, knowledge alone is not enough. While acquiring knowledge is crucial, its true power lies in the ability to apply it effectively. This chapter emphasizes the pivotal role of transforming knowledge into actionable strategies, underscoring that knowledge with action is the ultimate key to success in CA exams.

Knowledge Acquisition: The Foundation

The first step in your journey is the acquisition of knowledge. Through rigorous study, attending lectures, and understanding core concepts, you build a solid foundation. This knowledge equips you with the theoretical understanding necessary to tackle the complexities of the CA curriculum. However, knowledge, in isolation, remains dormant.

The Power of Application

Knowledge becomes powerful when put into action. It is through the application of learned concepts in real-world scenarios, practice problems, and exam simulations that you truly grasp and master the material. Here's how you can turn knowledge into action:

- Practical Problem-Solving: Engage in solving numerous practical problems. This not only reinforces your understanding but also hones your problem-solving skills.

- Case Studies and Simulations: Participate in case studies and simulations that mirror real-world challenges. This prepares you for practical application and critical thinking.

- Internships and Training: Gain hands-on experience through internships and training programs. Applying theoretical knowledge in a professional setting enhances your learning and skill development.

Continuous Improvement

The journey doesn't end with the exam. Continuous learning and improvement are vital. Reflect on your experiences, seek feedback, and stay updated with the latest industry trends. Engage in professional development and pursue advanced certifications to keep your knowledge relevant and impactful.

The Secret to Success

The secret to success in CA exams and beyond lies in the seamless integration of knowledge and action. By actively applying what you learn, you transform theoretical insights into practical expertise. This not only helps you excel in exams but also prepares you for a successful career as a Chartered Accountant.

Final Thoughts

As you close this chapter, remember that the true measure of your knowledge is in its application. Embrace every opportunity to turn your learning into action. This dynamic combination will empower you to achieve your goals, overcome challenges, and unlock your full potential as a successful CA professional. Keep learning, keep applying, and let your actions be the testament to your knowledge. ?

You've got what it takes to succeed. Best of luck on your journey to becoming a Chartered Accountant!

MOTIVATIONAL QUOTES FOR INSPIRATION

1. "The harder you work for something, the greater you'll feel when you achieve it."

2. "Success doesn't come from what you do occasionally, it comes from what you do consistently."

3. "Dream big. Start small. Act now."

4. "Your limitation—it's only your imagination."

5. "Push yourself, because no one else is going to do it for you."

6. "Sometimes later becomes never. Do it now."

7. "Great things never come from comfort zones."

8. "Dream it. Wish it. Do it."

9. "Success is not for the lazy."

10. "Wake up with determination. Go to bed with satisfaction."

11. "Do something today that your future self will thank you for."

12. "Little things make big days."

13. "It's going to be hard, but hard does not mean impossible."

14. "Don't stop when you're tired. Stop when you're done."

15. "The key to success is to start before you're ready."

16. "Believe you can and you're halfway there."

17. "The difference between ordinary and extraordinary is that little extra."

18. "Work hard in silence. Let success make the noise."

19. "The best view comes after the hardest climb."

20. "Success is what happens after you have survived all your mistakes."

21. "The only place where success comes before work is in the dictionary."

22. "Success is not in what you have, but who you are."

23. "The only limit to our realization of tomorrow will be our doubts of today."

24. "You don't have to be great to start, but you have to start to be great."

25. "Don't watch the clock; do what it does. Keep going."

26. "A dream doesn't become reality through magic; it takes sweat, determination, and hard work."

27. "Success is not the key to happiness. Happiness is the key to success. If you love what you are doing, you will be successful."

28. "Success usually comes to those who are too busy to be looking for it."

29. "Opportunities don't happen, you create them."

30. "Success is walking from failure to failure with no loss of enthusiasm."

31. "All progress takes place outside the comfort zone."

32. "Don't be afraid to give up the good to go for the great."

33. "I find that the harder I work, the more luck I seem to have."

34. "The road to success and the road to failure are almost exactly the same."

35. "Success is not how high you have climbed, but how you make a positive difference to the world."

36. "Keep your face always toward the sunshine—and shadows will fall behind you."

37. "Success is the sum of small efforts, repeated day in and day out."

38. "The way to get started is to quit talking and begin doing."

39. "Don't be pushed around by the fears in your mind. Be led by the dreams in your heart."

40. "The only place where your dream becomes impossible is in your own thinking."

41. "It always seems impossible until it's done."

42. "Your time is limited, so don't waste it living someone else's life."

43. "Do what you can with all you have, wherever you are."

44. "Hustle in silence and let your success make the noise."

45. "If you can dream it, you can achieve it."

46. "To see what is right and not do it is a lack of courage."

47. "Don't let what you cannot do interfere with what you can do."

48. "Success is not final, failure is not fatal: It is the courage to continue that counts."

49. "You are never too old to set another goal or to dream a new dream."

50. "The future belongs to those who believe in the beauty of their dreams."

51. "Hard times don't create heroes. It is during the hard times when the 'hero' within us is revealed."

52. "In the middle of every difficulty lies opportunity."

53. "Success seems to be connected with action. Successful people keep moving. They make mistakes but they don't quit."

54. "Life is 10% what happens to us and 90% how we react to it."

55. "Perseverance is not a long race; it is many short races one after the other."

56. "Every accomplishment starts with the decision to try."

57. "What you do today can improve all your tomorrows."

58. "The secret of success is to do the common thing uncommonly well."

59. "Success is where preparation and opportunity meet."

60. "Believe you can and you're halfway there."

61. "What seems to us as bitter trials are often blessings in disguise."

62. "The more you practice, the better you get, the more freedom you have to create."

63. "It's not about ideas. It's about making ideas happen."

64. "Success isn't just about what you accomplish in your life; it's about what you inspire others to do."

65. "You just can't beat the person who never gives up."

66. "Everything you've ever wanted is on the other side of fear."

67. "Success is liking yourself, liking what you do, and liking how you do it."

68. "Failure is another stepping stone to greatness."

69. "Success is about creating value."

70. "Challenges are what make life interesting and overcoming them is what makes life meaningful."

71. "The only way to do great work is to love what you do."

72. "Your passion is waiting for your courage to catch up."

73. "Small daily improvements over time lead to stunning results."

74. "Every day is an opportunity to get better. Don't waste it."

75. "The only thing standing between you and your goal is the story you keep telling yourself as to why you can't achieve it."

76. "Your greatest risk is in thinking too small."

77. "Take the risk or lose the chance."

78. "Focus on being productive instead of busy."

79. "Stop being afraid of what can go wrong and start being excited about what can go right."

80. "Success is not for the chosen few. Success is for the few who choose."

81. "Dream big dreams, then put on your overalls and go out and get to work."

82. "What we achieve inwardly will change outer reality."

83. "Never give up. Great things take time. Be patient."

84. "Don't count the days; make the days count."

85. "The secret to your success is found in your daily routine."

86. "You are what you repeatedly do. Excellence, then, is not an act, but a habit."

87. "Motivation is what gets you started. Habit is what keeps you going."

88. "The biggest risk is not taking any risk."

89. "If you get tired, learn to rest, not to quit."

90. "Keep going. Each step may get harder, but don't stop. The view is beautiful at the top."

91. "Success is not a destination; it is a journey."

92. "A winner is a dreamer who never gives up."

93. "Believe in yourself, take on your challenges, and dig deep within yourself to conquer fears."

94. "Difficult roads often lead to beautiful destinations."

95. "Success is not about the result, it's about what you learn along the way."

96. "With hard work, anything is possible."

97. "Turn your wounds into wisdom."

98. "Start where you are. Use what you have. Do what you can."

99. "Your potential is endless."

100. "What we achieve inwardly will change outer reality." - Plutarch

101. "The journey of a thousand miles begins with one step."

102. "Fall seven times, stand up eight." - Japanese Proverb

103. "The best way to predict your future is to create it." - Abraham Lincoln

104. "Do not wait to strike till the iron is hot; but make it hot by striking." - William Butler Yeats

105. "It does not matter how slowly you go as long as you do not stop." - Confucius

106."The harder the conflict, the more glorious the triumph." - Thomas Paine

107. "With patience, even the mulberry leaf becomes a silk gown." - Chinese Proverb

108. Run if you can, walk if you must, crawl if you need to, but never stop moving forward.

Keep these quotes close by to remind yourself that every effort you put in today brings you closer to your goal.These proverbs remind us that persistence, patience, and a positive mindset are key to achieving our goals. Keep pushing forward and believe in your ability to succeed! ???